Photography by Amy and Hans Rueffert

For my family and for my friends.

I am who I am because of you.

Thank you.

———◆———

You are who you are because of your family and friends.

Thank them.

———◆———

In memory of –

Sonja Yvonne Rueffert Walcott

1969-2004

Published by Luna7

Produced and printed by Graphic Innovations, LLC

Web address: www.graphicinv.com

Graphic design and layout by Kevin Powell

FIRST US EDITION PUBLISHED 2009

ISBN 978-1-60743-171-8

Eat like there's no tomorrow

Hans Rueffert

HJR

EAT WELL, BE WELL ... GESUNDHEIT

eat
like there's no Tomorrow

THE ADVOCATE COLLECTION

Hans Rueffert

Contents

hello

my name is Hans

Introduction

So before we get ahead of ourselves, let's sort out this "Never Trust a Skinny Chef" business.

I hear the questions: "Why is he so skinny?" and "Doesn't he eat his own cooking?" all the

time. The short answer: cancer. I was diagnosed with gastric cancer the day before my 33rd

birthday in 2005 and after multiple surgeries, chemo, and radiation therapy, I ended up losing

half of my stomach, half of my esophagus, and about 70 pounds. My cancer experience forever

changed the way I look at eating and the way that food makes us feel and I try to share those

epiphanies whenever possible. We'll talk more about that later, but for now… let's eat!

Like there's no To

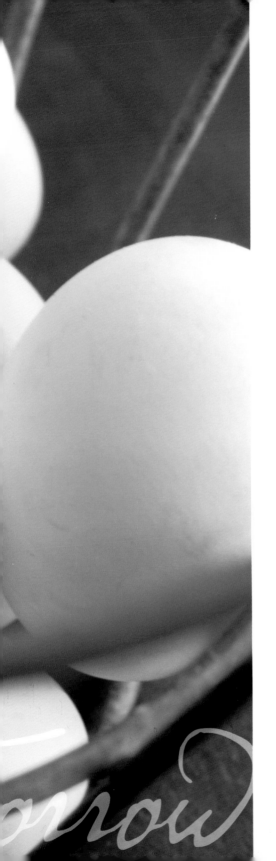

Like there's no tomorrow

If you knew you had one last meal, one final chance to take your place at the table with family and friends, what would you eat? What would your final menu look like? Would it look like a cartoon banquet, piled high with roasts and pies and mountains of pasta? Or would you swing through the Dairy Queen for one last banana split? Or would it be a simple plate of artesian cheeses and a handful of ripe figs?

One of my final meals with a full-sized stomach was at the original Ninfa's in Houston, the one near the stadium. My pending surgery was the elephant in the room, and we all ignored it as we constructed our sizzling fajitas, layering each tortilla with fresh salsa, sour cream, cilantro, and some of the best, grilled skirt steak I've ever experienced. I ate like a fool; loading tortilla after tortilla until the skillet was so clean a forensic team would find no clue of what we'd consumed. I thought of that meal often during the following eight weeks in the hospital, when my only source of nutrition came through a tube plugged directly into my intestines and the only thing I was allowed to "eat" was crushed ice, and even then in extremely limited quantity.

And it's that word, "quantity" that I was a bit preoccupied with at the time. Like so many of us in this country, I'd grown accustomed to eating as much as I wanted whenever I wanted, and losing a little more than half of my stomach meant that the days of all-you-can-eat feasts would soon become nothing more than a distant memory. But you know what? I don't miss those all-out, food-shoveling exercises in gluttony. My limited capacity for food has pushed my focus back to quality. I get excited about a simple piece of dense bread with butter and herring or a handful of black-eyed peas eaten fresh from the garden - simple foods, rich flavors, foods that connect me with my history, and foods that make me live for the future. Life is truly too short to eat poorly and I look forward to each meal as if it could truly be my last. Not in some morbid mindset, but in a way that celebrates not only the food, but the people who grow it, its preparation, and the family and friends we share it with.

On Recipes

I hate recipes. Well, that's not entirely accurate. I spend a good deal of my "free" time reading them. In fact, we have so many cookbooks in our house that I wonder from time to time if they're not reproducing when we're looking the other way. Piles of food magazines and books litter my favorite spots throughout the house. While my wife bathes the kids, I sneak downstairs to flip through my dog-eared Culinaria cookbooks to look up an answer to some burning kitchen curiosity. Later, when the kids are tucked in their beds, she reads historical tales of ancient Scotland while I drool over the latest issue of Gourmet, always inspired by Ruth Reichel's editor's letter. OK, so if I'm going to be completely honest with myself, I'd have to say that I do, in fact, love recipes.

But I do hate measuring things. I hate the sound those little metal teaspoon things make when they clang against each other. I hate the way the measuring cups stick in my kitchen gadget drawer. I resent the flour that sticks to the side of the container after I dump its contents in a bowl. My wife, on the other hand, loves these things. She loves the cute little spoons that measure a "dash" or a "smidgeon." She smiles as she carefully fills one of her many measuring cups with cream, her eyes squinting to make sure the liquid hits its line. It's a beautiful thing to watch her bake, and I envy that level of patience. But I still hate measuring things.

So the trick for me here is to force myself to quantify, or at least semi-quantify things that I simply do not measure in "real life." And so the recipes in this book, if you can call them that, are not hard, iron-clad rules by which you must prepare each dish. They're more like suggestions. I want you to take these ideas and make them your own. I've always believed that cooking is a bit like driving, and recipes are like your road map. There are a thousand ways to get from Point A to Point B. As long as you get where you intended to go, there really is no wrong way of getting there. If you find joy in dirtying a hundred little measuring cups and spoons along the way, go for it. If you just want to roll up your sleeves and throw a bunch of stuff in a pan, that's brilliant. Either way, find out what works best for you and make each dish your own.

On Ingredients

Here's a simple lesson I learned from my father that I'd like to pass along to you, and that is:

You can't make chicken salad out of chicken poop.

Of course, he used a more colorful four-letter word than the one I've chosen to share, but the message still rings true. You can't start with inferior ingredients and expect to end up with superior food. At the same time, if you consistently use quality ingredients, cooking is a breeze. It's hard to make good ingredients taste bad. I mean, it takes effort! So as you set out to prepare your next meal, have a good look at what's in your pantry. If it's questionable, outdated, or unidentifiable, throw it away. Then head out to your local gourmet shop or market and stock up on the good stuff. Let me be the first to confirm that life's too short to eat, or cook with, anything but the good stuff.

Asparagus

In life, it's always fun to have something to look forward to. When we were younger, my sister and I would count down the days until our birthdays or Christmas or Easter or Halloween (I still count the days to Halloween!). As my obsession with food evolved, each flip of the calendar hinted at some new seasonal food to anticipate. Every month held its own treasures: okra in June, chanterelles in July, peaches in August, apples in October and so on. The food season really begins in early spring with the emergence of asparagus. Mature asparagus plants break through the chilly soil with an amazing intensity, each stalk racing skyward to open their ferny fronds and drink in the sun. The early shoots are harvested before they have a chance to unfurl and, for a few short weeks, these harbingers of spring find their way onto my plate at nearly every meal.

If you ever get the chance to visit Germany in the spring, you'll find a country that's absolutely obsessed with asparagus. And we're not talking a mild infatuation here. No, we're talking full-on infatuation, with every restaurant and market heralding the arrival of the year's first bundles of pale spears. While they do eat green asparagus, it's the white asparagus that ignites the country's obsession. The asparagus are grown in long rows of rich soil that's been mounded up to keep the spears from the sunlight that would eventually turn the stalks green. Using special, long knives, harvesters cut the stalks below the soil right before the tips pierce the surface to meet the light. The albino spears are eaten simply steamed or broiled and served with thinly sliced ham and Hollandaise sauce.

In general, you can use white and green (and even purple!) asparagus interchangeably, but you will sometimes stumble on spears with woody, fibrous lower stalks. On thicker stalks, you may need to peel the lower portion of each stalk with a vegetable peeler or paring knife. You can also use the "bendy" trick to find where the tender part of each stalk begins. As you hold the stalks near the bottom between your thumbs and forefingers, start trying to bend the stalks. Keep inching your way up the stalks, bending at each time until the stalks naturally snap. Anything from that point up is tender; anything below the snap is fibrous. You can save those woody bases for soups if you're so inclined, or save them for the compost pile.

Asparagus Salad with Lemon Yogurt Vinaigrette

Grilling lemons may not be something you're used to doing, but it adds a lush, caramel sweetness to the dressing. If you're using a grill pan, cooking the asparagus after the lemons will add a little extra zing to the spears.

3 lemons, halved
1 tablespoon olive oil
6-8 asparagus spears
1 ½ tablespoons white balsamic vinegar
2 teaspoons Dijon mustard
1 garlic clove, minced
salt & pepper
¼ cup plain yogurt
2-3 cups fresh arugula
2-3 tablespoons fresh goat cheese (chevre)
lemon zest

Grill the lemons pulp side down on medium heat, rotating them occasionally so that they don't burn. When they've softened up a bit and have some nice color on them, set the lemons to the side and let them rest while you work on the asparagus. Add the oil to the pan and sauté/grill the asparagus over medium heat for about 2-3 minutes. The asparagus should be warm throughout, but still crunchy. How can you tell if they're ready? Eat one!

To make the dressing, use a fork to really render out the juice and pulp from the grilled lemons. Add vinegar, mustard, yogurt, garlic, salt, and pepper. Whisk to combine. Arrange the arugula in a bowl. Crumble the goat cheese over the arugula in a large bowl and add your dressing. Toss the salad thoroughly, plate, and arrange the asparagus on top. Add a sprinkle of lemon zest and a little cracked pepper and you're good to go.

Pork Schnitzel
ala Holstein Asparagus

There's just something about fresh asparagus with runny egg yolks, and place all of that on top of a nice schnitzel and you've really got something special. You would traditionally bread the cutlet in breadcrumbs, but I like the nutty crunch of the wheat germ in this preparation.

1 tablespoon oil
2 tablespoons butter, divided
¼ cup whole wheat, all-purpose flour
salt & pepper
1 3-4 oz. pork cutlet, pounded flat
4 eggs
½ cup wheat germ
4 asparagus spears

Add the oil and 1 tablespoon of butter to a skillet on medium-high heat. Put the flour on a large plate and season with salt and pepper. Pour the wheat germ on another large plate. Crack two of the eggs in a wide bowl and whisk thoroughly. Now, dredge the pork in the seasoned flour, then dip in the beaten eggs, then dredge in the wheat germ. Make sure you're totally coating the pork and that now wet spots are exposed. If you're doing multiple schnitzels, go ahead and bread them all while your hands are messy. Now, wash your hands! To sauté schnitzel(s), place the pork in the skillet away from you so that the hot butter/oil mixture doesn't splatter back and burn you. Cook the pork about 2 minutes per side until they're nice and golden brown. If the pan's not too crowded you can just sauté the asparagus while you're cooking the pork. Alternatively, remove the browned schnitzels and let them rest on a paper towel lined plate while you quickly sauté the asparagus spears. In a separate pan, add your other tablespoon of butter and cook the two remaining eggs the way you like them. I like mine just over easy so that there's still enough runny yolk to get all friendly with the asparagus. To serve, first plate the schnitzel, then the spears on top of that, and finally the eggs on top of that. Season with a little salt and pepper and, if you have some, a few curls of good Parmesan cheese.

Feeling Fresh

What do you consider to be "fresh" food? Is it food that's been recently removed from its cellophane wrapper? Or is it food that hasn't yet passed its printed expiration date? With planes flying produce in from every corner of every continent, we've been led to believe that "fresh" means beautiful, yet tasteless strawberries from the southern hemisphere or pale hothouse tomatoes that haven't seen the sun in weeks. . The truth is, most market "fresh" produce was picked anywhere from one to three weeks earlier, often before it was ripe, trucked, packaged, gassed, refrigerated, trucked again and then finally displayed on your grocer's shelves. Just because we can import food from all over the world doesn't necessarily mean we should. The fruits and vegetables that haunt most mega-stores are selected and bred for their shelf life and their ability to be transported without injury. Flavor and nutrition are forced to take a backseat to these economic considerations.

Now don't get me wrong; I'd rather folks eat these out-of-season fruits and vegetables than none at all. I'll be the first to admit that I'd rather see Chilean grapes in the winter than go without until mid-summer. Being a stomach cancer survivor, I'm hyper-aware of the importance of including ample daily doses of fruits and vegetables in your diet. What I'd like to propose and encourage here is that once you've tasted truly farm-fresh, locally-produced foods, you'll quickly understand that anything else simply pales in comparison. Eat a handful of sun-warmed muscadines off the vine, slice into a mottled heirloom tomato or crack into a pecan underneath the branches of its parent tree and you'll experience a paradigm shift in food that is hard to recover from. You'll find yourself stalking your local farmers' market at 7:30 on a Saturday (didn't I used to sleep late on Saturdays?), jockeying in line with your fellow foodies to get a chance at the best the season has to offer.

Lucky for us all, the trend toward farm-fresh, local food is gaining momentum. After decades of eating processed, pre-packaged foods, consumers are getting back to the basics. I applaud the large manufacturers who are following this trend, but I can't help but laugh when I hear their "Now 100 Percent Natural!" commercials. Now 100 percent natural? What the hell were you feeding us before? Was there really a time when we felt that eating someone's science project was better than eating fresh, real food? Were we actually hornswagled into

believing that margarine (which is one hydrogen atom away from being plastic) is better than pure, natural, churned butter? I'll try not to get on my soapbox here (though I'll warn you that I might step on the soapbox from time to time), but I will say that it's about time we recognized that what we eat directly affects the way we feel. If you eat processed, you'll feel processed. In contrast, if you make the switch to eating fresh, vibrant foods, you'll be amazed at how quickly you'll start to feel fresh and vibrant.

I call Georgia my home state, and we Georgians are especially lucky when it comes to food. Our diverse geography and rich agricultural history offer us enough variety to sustain and inspire even the most demanding consumer. The state's fecundity is irrefutable and known across the country (and even internationally) for its unique and consistently excellent foods. Peaches, pecans, Vidalia onions, blueberries, peanuts, apples, sorghum, okra, corn, muscadines and more are waiting for you to enjoy. And while our coast here in Georgia may be relatively small, it's lush with wild shrimp, blue crabs, fish and clams. I had a chance to explore the state's culinary treasures while creating the *Hans Cooks the South* television series and learned more about Georgia and our local harvest than I ever would have guessed. There are some passionate people producing food in this country and you can find them if you just go out and look.

While many of the foods in this collection are from Georgia, the underlying premise here rings true no matter where you live. Food becomes inspiration when you follow it to its source, exploring each ingredient as it springs from the ground or drops from a tree or is pulled from the sea. It would take several lifetimes to see and taste all the foods the world has to offer, so start locally. Like me, you may be surprised to learn what's being grown and harvested in your home state.

Ramps

A few warm days in the spring and I'm ready to go ramp hunting! The word hunting may not be appropriate here as it connotes rifles or arrows or at the very least, some sense of participation on the side of the hunted. But given their limited and very specific growing requirements, ramp hunting can be somewhat of a strenuous sport. Ramps are the wild allium (think hyper-garlic) that grows throughout the eastern United States during a brief time in early spring. We get them in the high elevations of the North Georgia mountains in early to mid-April before the trees fully leaf out. Ramps have a rich history in Appalachia and were even thought to ward off evil spirits and vampires, but they're more likely to just ward off any chances of good breath. Locals typically eat them pickled and fried, most commonly cooked with eggs or "taters" or both. Unfortunately, many of the locals only eat the bulbs of the ramp and discard the greens. The greens are quite possibly my favorite part as they taste like garlic-kissed spinach and can be used to add that garlic kick to more subtle dishes. The bulbs will let you know in a hurry that they're there, while the greens just sneak that distinct garlicky flavor into whatever they grace.

Once you find a patch of ramps (or "mess o'ramps"), it's a sight to behold. You can walk in the mountains for hours and not see a single ramp and then come across an area that's nearly infested with them. If the breeze is right, you can actually smell them before you see them. I'd heard about ramps my whole life but was only inducted to the ramp culture recently. I must say I look forward to them now and even my young son Finn gets excited about the possibility of ramps and eggs. We saw ramps for sale in a farmer's market during a family visit to Germany. They're called Bärlauch in German, which means "Bear's Leek," presumably because bears have good taste and enjoy them just as much as we do. If nothing else, ramps give you an excuse to get up in the mountains and enjoy a good walk. We've met ramp hunters on our forages that will admit that they're really not big fans of eating them but they go year after year with their friends just for the sheer pleasure of getting outside and doing something. Those are the kind of people I need to hook up with so I can graciously take the spoils of their foraging.

Ramp Butter

This is a great way to preserve the flavor of ramps well beyond their growing season. It makes a great topping for steaks, chops, fish, and even grilled vegetables. If you can't find ramps, try using 5 cloves of garlic and a handful of fresh spinach.

8-10 ramps
1 tablespoon olive oil
1 teaspoon salt
½ teaspoon pepper
½ teaspoon grated nutmeg
1 lb. unsalted butter, at room temperature
parchment paper

Wash the ramps thoroughly to remove all traces of the forest, then separate bulbs from the greens. Add the olive oil to a medium pan and sauté bulbs until they're just translucent, about 2-3 minutes. Rough chop the greens and add them to the bulbs. Sauté the ramps for another minute or so until the greens just begin to wilt. Season with the salt, pepper, and nutmeg and put the whole mess into the food processor. Pulse the processor until the greens are all chopped and reach the consistency of pesto. Allow the ramp puree to cool to room temperature before smashing in with your room temperature butter. You can use a mixer for this, but I like to use my hands to really squish it all into the butter. Lay the butter lengthwise in the middle of a large sheet of parchment paper and roll the whole thing up like a giant saltwater taffy. Twist the ends tightly to really force the butter into a nice uniform log. Now freeze the butter until you need it. When you want some of that ramp flavor, just slice of what you need and put the rest back in the freezer for later.

Ramp Soup

When you're eating a soup this simple, smooth and delicious, it's hard to imagine that ramps could've ever had a bad reputation! Use this as a jumping on point, embellishing as you like with things like artichokes, potatoes, or celeriac. In my mind, soup should never be made the same way twice …

2 cups vegetable stock
6-8 ramps
1 tablespoon olive oil
1 Vidalia onion
1 teaspoon flour
1 cup whole milk
1 cups heavy cream
2 tablespoons sour cream
salt & pepper
½ teaspoon nutmeg

Pour the stock in a heavy pot and heat it until it's hot, but not boiling. Wash the ramps thoroughly (always a good idea) and rough chop them. Place the ramps in a food processor, add a ladle of the hot stock, a pinch of salt, and then puree until the ramps are thoroughly processed. In another pot, heat the olive oil over medium high heat and add the Vidalia onion, salt, pepper, and nutmeg. Sauté the onion until it's just translucent, then sprinkle in the flour and give it all a good stir. Now, add your pureed ramps, milk, sour cream, stock and heavy cream and bringing the soup to a quick boil. Remove from heat and serve. I like to serve each portion with a dollop of sour cream and a sprig of fresh thyme.

How local is local?

The "localvore" movement makes sense on so many levels. Not only are you eating food that is hyper-fresh, you're also reducing the amount of petroleum used in both packaging and transporting foods from other regions. I happen to live in a part of northwest Georgia that puts me about an hour drive from Alabama, Tennessee and both of the Carolinas. Folks in South Georgia may be closer to northern Florida farms, so their local is certainly different from mine. You may live on the border of another country altogether! So rather than trying to define local in terms of some agreed-upon distance from your home, just be mindful of the fact that the foods grown closer are usually fresher, more flavorful and vibrant than foods transported in from places far away. Let me say again that I'm not proposing some radical isolationist method of eating, but I am suggesting that we eat foods produced close to home whenever possible.

My spice cabinet is full of treasures from all over the world and I'm always on the lookout for more. Things like cinnamon, nutmeg, ginger, cardamom and the like may not be native to our region, but they work wonderfully with the items that do call the South home. Similarly, fresh Hawaiian pineapple partners wonderfully with Georgia's sweet white shrimp or even tossed in with a handful of fresh-picked blueberries. A little of the world's exotic flavors can make local food sing with new and often exciting tones, so don't be afraid of a little experimentation. After all, that's largely what cooking is … one kitchen experiment after another.

Blueberries

What is it about blueberries that make them so universally adored? I have strong childhood memories of plucking wild berries and squishing them between my teeth. My Uncle once tried to pay me to gather wild blueberries so that my Aunt could make jam. I returned from several hours foraging with a near-empty basket, a swollen belly and blue stained teeth. As a toddler, my son Finn would shamble around the house saying "Boo-bay, boo-bay!" until we'd refill his little berry bowl. It's just hard to be unhappy when you have blueberries.

For me, blueberries strike the perfect balance of sweet and tart, all neatly wrapped up in a bite-size gem. Blueberries are experiencing somewhat of a renaissance at the moment, thanks largely in part to nutritional science's reports on the amazing health properties of the berry. Loaded with antioxidants, blueberries have been shown to inhibit the growth of cancer cells as well as repair damaged brain cells. And the best news is that frozen berries seem to retain all of these impressive health qualities. Of course there's nothing like wolfing down fresh berries, but when the season ends frozen berries can step in to ease your blues. Frozen berries can be added to oatmeal and other cereals, baked goods, or yogurt smoothies.

Typically when we think about blueberries we think of Michigan or Maine. But we Georgians are lucky to have a growing blueberry industry in the southern part of the state. My blueberry quest brought me to a little town near Brunswick called Nahunta. What's really special about Nahunta is that much of the blueberry crop is grown on land that was once used to cultivate tobacco. How's that for a health turnaround? Nahunta's blueberry crop comes in a few weeks earlier than the rest of the state, starting with fruits from the Southern High Bush and then following with Rabbit Eye berries. To the west of Nahunta you'll find Alma, the official blueberry capital of Georgia. If you find yourself near either of these cities while the berries are in season, do yourself a favor and stop in for a treat you'll never forget.

Blueberry Orange Clafouti

There's no wrong way to eat blueberries and I find myself incorporating them into salad dressings and chutneys as well as desserts. One of my favorite ways to enjoy them is baked in a clafouti, a rustic French dish that sits on the fence between a custard and a pancake. Traditionally a clafouti is made with cherries (which is also delicious), but the sweet tartness of the blueberries work marvelously. You can also mix seasonal fruits if you like. This recipe is fairly bulletproof, so feel free to tweak it to your liking. Served hot or cold, with ice cream or whipped cream, this stuff will make you smile. Just a warning: your teeth may be blue!

2 cups blueberries, fresh or frozen
1 ¼ cups whole milk
⅓ cup + 4 tablespoons raw sugar
Finely grated zest of one large orange
1 teaspoon vanilla extract
3 large eggs pinch of salt
1 cup of all-purpose unbleached flour
mint to garnish

Preheat the oven to 375 degrees F (or 190 deg C). Preheat a glass or other ovenproof baking dish while you prepare the batter. Alternatively, you could use individual ramekins for single-sized servings.
In a large bowl, whisk together the milk, orange zest, ⅓ cup sugar, vanilla, eggs, salt and flour. Remove the heated dish and add the blueberries straight to the dish. Sprinkle with the remaining raw sugar. Evenly distribute the milk/egg mixture over the berries. Quickly return to the oven for 35 to 40 minutes until puffed up, golden and cooked through. Serve warm or at room temperature and garnish with a sprig of fresh mint. If you'd prefer, you can bake the clafoutis in individual servings sized ramekins. Please note that the cooking time will be a little l ess for individual sized servings.

Blueberry Cornbread

This might sound a little strange, but trust me on this one. The sweetness of the berries really complements the natural sugars in the cornmeal. Do yourself a favor and seek out stone-ground meal. I'm lucky to have a few grist mills in my neck of the woods, but if you look in the health food section of your favorite market, you'll find what you're looking for.

nonstick cooking spray
½ cup flour
1 ½ cups cornmeal
1 teaspoon salt
1 teaspoon sugar
1 tablespoon baking powder
3 large eggs, room temperature
1 ¼ cups low-fat milk, room temperature
8 tablespoons (one stick) unsalted butter, melted
½ cup fresh blueberries

Preheat the oven to 400°F. Coat a 9" x 9" pan with nonstick spray or butter. In a mixing bowl, sift the together the flour, cornmeal, salt, sugar and baking powder. Gently stir in the eggs, milk and butter with a wooden spoon until the dry ingredients are just moistened. Do not over mix or the end result may be dense and chewy. Gently fold in the blueberries.

Pour the batter into the pan and bake for about 15 minutes or until the edges are golden brown around the edges. The cornbread is done when a small knife inserted in the center comes out dry. Serve with a swipe of butter and a drizzle of local honey.

Blueberry-Peach-Vidalia Onion Chutney

Chutney is somewhat like a jam, but typically includes not only sweet flavors, but salty, sour, and sometimes spicy as well. This is a great way to incorporate produce that may be passing its prime (overripe fruits are excellent in this recipe) or to utilize and preserve an abundant harvest. This chutney combines three Georgia favorites and is downright tasty.

4 cups blueberries, fresh or frozen
4 peaches, seeded and diced
1 large sweet onion (Vidalia!)
1 ½ cups red wine vinegar
½ cup golden raisins
½ cup brown sugar
2 teaspoons mustard seed
1 tablespoon candied ginger
½ teaspoon cinnamon
1 teaspoon salt
½ teaspoon grated nutmeg
1 teaspoon olive oil
1 small red chili diced (optional)

In a large, non-reactive skillet on medium-high heat, add olive oil, onions, mustard seed, ginger, cinnamon, salt, nutmeg, and diced chili (if using) and sweat the ingredients for about 2 minutes. Add your blueberries, raisins, peaches, and vinegar and reduce heat to medium. When peaches become somewhat soft, add the sugar and reduce the heat to a simmer. Continue to simmer, stirring occasionally, for about 45 minutes or until chutney is at your preferred thickness.

The chutney will keep well covered and refrigerated for 2-3 weeks. Try it on duck, pork, chicken, beef, or game meats like venison. It also makes a fantastic sandwich spread.

Blue & Blue Salad

Watercress is one of my favorite greens, especially when its inherent peppery notes are paired with something tart or sweet. Blending the rind of the blue cheese in with the dressing lends a lush creaminess that's reminiscent of a good Greek dressing. Beautiful crunch, beautiful colors and blueberries that pop in your mouth like caviar.

4-5 oz. blue cheese
5 tablespoon blueberry butter or jam
2 cups watercress
½ teaspoon salt
¼ cup fresh blueberries plus more for garnishing
½ teaspoon coarse ground black pepper
4 tablespoons white balsamic vinegar
8 tablespoons olive oil
1 cup red cabbage slivers (plus outer leaves for presentation)

I like to use a nice slice of blue cheese and separate the rind from the more crumbly center. Reserve the crumbly bits for garnishing the salad at the end.

In a food processor, combine the rind portion of the cheese, blueberry butter, salt, ¼ cup blueberries, pepper, vinegar, & oil. Pulse together until the dressing is smooth and creamy.

Now simply combine the watercress, shaved red cabbage, and enough dressing to gently coat it all. Garnish with blueberries and blue cheese crumbles. I like to serve the salad in one of the cupped outer leaves of the red cabbage. Any remaining dressing can be used as a tart dip for crudités.

The Raulerson's Blue Ribbon Blueberry Kuchen

Michele and Tom Raulerson are known throughout Georgia for their award-winning beef jerky (www.circlerjerky.com), but it turns out they also know their way around the kitchen with a pile of blueberries. I was honored to be a judge at the Taste of Nahunta festival and, while it was tough to choose a clear winner out of a dozen or so delicious blueberry-studded desserts, this particular entry scored highest on all the judges scorecards. So here's that award-winning recipe, straight from the Raulersons ... good stuff!

For the base:
1 cup all-purpose flour
2 tablespoons sugar
Pinch of salt
½ cup butter or margarine, softened
1 tablespoon white vinegar

For the filling:
2 tablespoons all-purpose flour
1 Cup sugar
1/8 teaspoon ground cinnamon
3 cups fresh blueberries, divided
Powdered sugar

Combine first 3 ingredients; cut in butter with pastry blender (we do it by hand) until mixture resembles coarse meal. Sprinkle vinegar evenly over surface; stir with fork until all dry ingredients are moistened. Press pastry in bottom of 9" spring form pan and up 1" on the sides of pan. Combine 2 tablespoons flour, 1 cup sugar, and cinnamon, mixing well. Stir in 2 cups blueberries; spread evenly over pastry. Bake at 400° F for 45 minutes. Remove from oven and sprinkle remaining 1 cup berries evenly over top. Chill well before removing from pan. Sprinkle with powdered sugar and serve with mint sprig and fresh berries on the side.

Lazy Girl
Fruit Cobbler

My wife Amy makes her "Lazy Girl Cobbler" all summer long using whatever we have on hand. The beauty of it is that we never have the same thing twice and no matter what variety she makes, it never stays around for long.

3 or 4 cups of fruit (blueberries, plums, peaches, or any combination of fresh or frozen fruit)
1 cup buttermilk 1 cup all purpose flour (unbleached)
1 cup raw sugar
2 tablespoons butter, cut into chips
2 tablespoons brown sugar

Preheat your oven to 350° F. Cover the bottom of a baking dish with the fruit. Mix together the buttermilk, flour, and 1 cup sugar and pour evenly over the fruit. Distribute the butter chips across the top of the mix, then sprinkle the whole thing with brown sugar. Bake for 45 minutes and enjoy either hot or cold. A good scoop of vanilla bean ice cream makes the whole thing a little less lazy, but it's worth the extra effort.

Along came cancer...

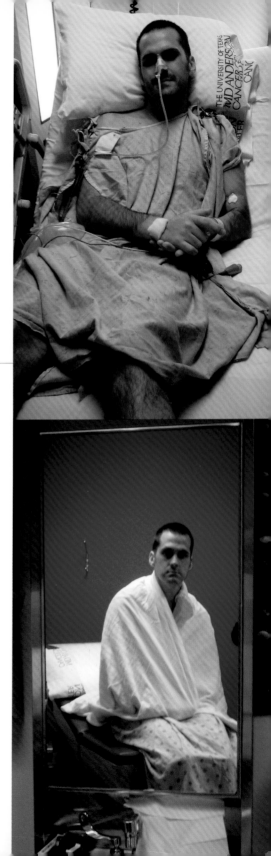

I'm a huge fan of irony. The same PBS station that introduced me to cooking shows also brought me to the doorsteps of British comedy classics like Benny Hill and Monty Python. On Saturday nights when service at the Inn was finished, I'd detoxify the evening's stress by giving myself over to an hour or so of brilliant British silliness. So the irony of a chef being diagnosed with stomach cancer was certainly not lost on me.

Just two short weeks after the Next Food Network Star finale, I found myself at work back in Ellijay. I had already shot the 'desk' portion of the day's news and was sitting at my computer trying to edit the show. For some reason, I found myself completely confused. It wasn't that I was having difficulties with some new challenge, but instead, I was confused by everything. I couldn't even figure out which button on my mouse was the left one and which one was the right. At the same time, my brain felt like it was trying to go to sleep. Not a sleepy type sleep, but a deep, uncontrollable, unshakable, bottom-of-the-ocean type sleep. After a bit of stubbornness on my part, I finally conceded that I needed to see a doctor. My friend Karen offered ... no ... insisted that someone drive me, but I was delusional enough to think I could drive the 15 miles to the hospital on my own (which is something that Karen still gives me grief about).

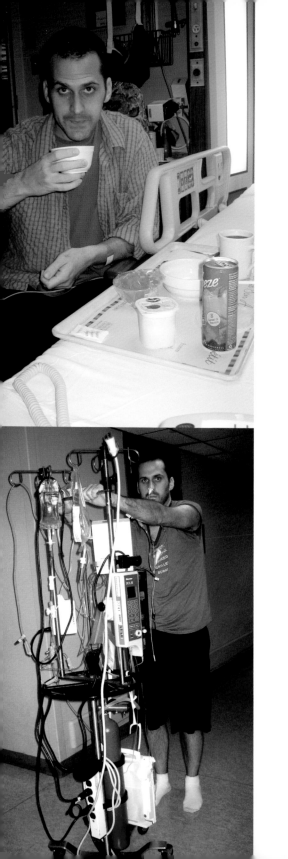

About 8 miles into the drive, my mind was so mushy that I finally decided to pull over and dial 911. Despite my best efforts, I was falling asleep. I remember the ambulance arriving, I remember the paramedic helping me into the vehicle, and I remember him smiling as he jabbed the IV in my arm and saying, "Man, you got SCREWED on the Food Network!" My dad followed the ambulance to the hospital and Amy was driving like a woman possessed to meet us there in the ER. All I wanted to do was sleep, but my overzealous paramedic friend wasn't having it.

At the hospital, blood tests revealed that my blood level was dangerously low. The first doctor said I should eat more red meat. The second (perhaps more intelligent) doctor said that I must be bleeding internally. The next day an endoscopy confirmed that suspicion. Just below the junction of my esophagus and my stomach lived a tumor… and it was bleeding. A biopsy confirmed what I somehow already knew… cancer. Stomach cancer.

We made the decision to put my health in the hands of Dr. York at Piedmont Hospital in Atlanta working closely with surgeons at the MD Anderson Cancer Hospital in Houston, Texas. In surgery, they found that the cancer had spread upward, so they yanked out half of my stomach and the lower half of my esophagus. The remaining lower portion of my stomach was pulled up and attached to the remaining upper portion of my esophagus. For seven weeks, the guy whose every thought was food, went without it. My nutrition was pumped into my intestines through a J-tube and the only thing I was allowed to eat was ice, and not much of it. The whole experience was grueling … extremely painful, extremely scary. (If you're interested in reading those experiences in detail, I kept an online journal which can be found at http://hansrue.livejournal.com/ and on my current blog: www.hansrue.blogspot.com)But if Nietzsche is to be believed and that which doesn't kill us truly does make us stronger, then there is a silver lining to my cancer experience. It's a tired cliché, but it's true: cancer gives its survivors a new set of eyes with which to view the world. I don't think you can truly appreciate your life until you almost lose it. I honestly believe that my family, my friends, and the kindness of strangers helped me pull through some very dark days.

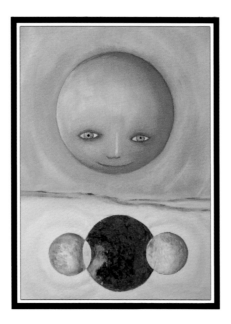

I started collecting notes in the hospital for a new cooking show idea, not knowing if I'd ever feel well enough to tackle such a project. In 2006, after chemotherapy, radiation, and 8 months worth of recovery, that idea became a reality and *Hans Cooks the World* was born. The show was an important part of my rehabilitation. If you watch the show sequentially you can watch my health improve as the show progresses. That show opened the door for *Hans Cooks the South*, a show produced by my friends at ETC for my new friends at Georgia Public Broadcasting. That show, in turn, was the catalyst that brought about this book. It's important to have goals when you're dealing with a potentially terminal illness. I think it sends our bodies a message that there's more living yet to do. I'm too busy to die!

Whether we'd care to admit it or not, cancer survivors tend to think in terms of not IF the cancer will return, but WHEN. Not a day passes where I don't question the future and if there will even be one for me. Rather than getting mired in those dark thoughts, I try to use those emotions as fuel. I try and treat each day as if it were my last, while cramming as much as I can into tomorrow. Ultimately, no matter when you check out, our ride on this planet is a short one. If nothing else, cancer makes you want to continue fighting to stay on that ride.

Atlantic Catch

I traveled to Darien, Ga. to get some video footage of a shrimp boat hauling in its catch. My first trip to this historic coastal town was a few months earlier in April during their annual Blessing of the Fleet festival, but the shrimp just weren't cooperating. I guess no one told the shrimp we were coming … or perhaps they did! You really don't need an excuse to visit Darien, one of Georgia's many coastal gems.

Captain Fred Todd agreed to take us "hill people" to experience a day on a commercial shrimp boat. We boarded the Sundown at about 4 a.m. and headed out beyond Sapelo Island. The pre-dawn sky was inky black save for brilliant flashes of heat lightning on the horizon. The sun finally made an appearance around 6 a.m. and it was a sunrise worth waking up for. The sun rises (or, to be a bit more accurate, the world turns towards the sun) every single day without fail, but it's still breathtaking to see those colors emerge and wash out the night sky. One of the effects of my cancer surgeries is that I can no longer physically vomit. I can still gag and be queasy and such, but those muscles that allow you to upchuck are no longer a part of my anatomy. I mention this because this was my first experience getting seasick since my innards have been remodeled. I leaned over the edge of the bow out of habit, but of course nothing came up. I just gagged for about three minutes and then the sensation was gone.

I didn't really feel solid until breakfast was served shortly after sunrise. The ship's striker (a term for the person in charge of the nets on board) was a man named Reed and he knew his way around the kitchen on the Sundown. Shrimp with bacon and gravy over grits is not what you'd usually think of for breakfast, but this was no ordinary day. The meal was simple, but incredibly flavorful and seemed to inspire a restorative effect on my heretofore shaky constitution. It was still delicious two hours later when the gravy was cold and the grits had transformed into one solid mass.

After several passes with the nets, Captain Todd decided to cut his losses and head in with about 80 pounds of shrimp in the keep. The ever-increasing price of diesel fuel has made this already fragile industry even more unstable. I left the Sundown with sea legs and a strong appreciation for the work those shrimpers do. It's tough work with an increasingly slim profit margin and a sometimes fickle catch. I don't think I'll look at shrimp the same way again.

I came to Darien in search of shrimp, but discovered so much more. The tidal marshes that make up much of the landscape are home to some of the cleanest waters in the country, a quality that reflects in the seafood grown and harvested there. You would not believe the variety: amazing clams, soft-shell crabs, oysters, whelks, and even world-class caviar harvested from local sturgeon. Beautiful place, amazing people, and amazing, well-managed seafood.

Shrimp Parfait

I love the simple, sweet tomato shrimp cocktails you find a good Mexican restaurants, and I adore fresh tomatillo salsa. This is a surprisingly vibrant combination of those two flavors and makes for a beautiful presentation.

2 cups water
1 cup shrimp, peeled and deveined
2 bay leaves
½ teaspoon peppercorns
½ teaspoon fennel seed
½ cup organic ketchup
½ cup vidalia onions
hot sauce (optional)
4-5 tomatillos
1 clove garlic, rough chopped
1 jalapeno pepper
juice from 2 limes
¼ cup cilantro, roughly torn
dollop of sour cream, to garnish

Add the water, shrimp, bay leaves, peppercorns, and fennel seed to a heavy pot. Poach the shrimp on low heat (make sure the water never reaches a boil) until they just turn pink and opaque. Drain the shrimp and shock them in a bowl of ice water. When they're nice and chilled, drain them again and rough chop the shrimp into bite size pieces. Divide the chopped shrimp into two equal piles.

For Red Sauce: In a bowl mix ketchup, onions, a splash of water, and half the shrimp together.
Add a splash of hot sauce if desired.

For Green Sauce: Grill the tomatillos and the jalapeno for about 2-3 minutes, turning frequently. You want the tomatillos to get a little soft and squishy. In a food processor, pulse the tomatillos, garlic, and jalapeno together until they're thoroughly pureed. Add the lime juice and cilantro then blend for another 10 seconds or so. Remove from the processor and add the remaining shrimp.

Keep everything nice and chilled until you're ready to assemble the parfaits. When you're ready to serve, simply alternate layers of the green and red cocktails. Feel free to add embellishments like sour cream, more diced onions or tortilla chips.

Clams with Garlic & Mint

Fresh clams are so delicious on their own, but a bit of wine, garlic, and mint really make them sing. This is the kind of food that I'll burn my fingers on while trying to fish them straight out of the pan. Delicious …

2 cloves garlic, roughly chopped
¼ cup dry white wine
½ stick butter, softened
2-3 pounds fresh clams
½ cup fresh mint, roughly chopped

Put the garlic, wine, butter, and clams in a wide, heavy pot with a heavy lid. Over medium heat, steam clams for a total of 5-7 minutes, checking them every few minutes and giving them a good stir. All of the clams should pop open on their own, so discard any that failed to open. They're no fun anyway. Spoon liquid from pan over all the clams and top with the chopped mint. You can put them in a fancy bowl, but I've usually eaten half of them by the time I get the bowl out of the cupboard.

Honey Cumin Shrimp with Okra

This is quite possibly my favorite way to eat shrimp. The whole thing comes together in minutes, so be sure not to overcook the okra or the shrimp. Try this over wild rice or quinoa.

1 tablespoon olive oil
2 cloves of garlic, sliced
½ cup diced Vidalia onions
1 teaspoon ground cumin
1 cup okra, sliced
1 cup shrimp
salt & pepper
1 teaspoon hot sauce (I love Sriracha, but Tabasco would work just fine)
1 tablespoon honey
½ cup wild rice, cooked

Add oil, garlic, onions, and cumin to a pan and let cook for 1 minute over medium high heat. Add the okra, shrimp, salt, pepper, and hot sauce and cook just until the shrimp turn pink. Drizzle with the honey and give it all a good toss.

The case for Organic and Transitional foods

My experience with gastric cancer has refined and often reshaped the way I look at food. Foods have tremendous impact on the way we feel, both mentally and physically. Reduced to its components, food is essentially fuel, but when I think of it that way, it loses much of its charm and romance. So I try and talk about food and health without hitting people over the head with gobs of science that's either intimidating or simply off-putting. I do tend to use the terms organic and transitional quite often, so I wanted spend a little time on those terms and how they relate to the foods we consume and to the planet we call home.

Organic

The term organic may not be as straightforward as you might think. Of course you'll remember from biology that any carbon-based material is considered organic, but in the context of food (and all food is organic by that standard), the term refers to the methods with which the food was raised or produced. Simply stated, organic foods were produced without the use of hormones, antibiotics, chemical pesticides, herbicides, artificial fertilizers, radiation, or genetic modification. To be Certified Organic, the farmer or food producer must pass an increasingly thorough and costly government certification process. The costs associated with both the organic methods of farming and the certification fees are passed along to the consumer, making Certified Organic products more expensive at the market. But is it worth it?

There's plenty of evidence that the epidemic overuse of certain pesticides, herbicides, chemical fertilizers and such are compromising not only human health, but the health of the planet as a whole. This being a cookbook, I don't want to start spouting alarmist statistics and depressing (though thought-provoking) environmental studies...there's plenty of resources, in print or online, for that kind of information. But even without that kind of hard evidence, the decision to go organic (whenever possible) was a natural one (no pun intended ... or was it?). I would never intentionally feed a spoonful of pesticides to my young children, so why would I buy chemical-laden foods for them if a suitable alternative were available. I would never give my children bovine growth hormones, so why give them hormone-rich milk when an organic alternative sits one shelf away from the conventional stuff. It's a decision that just feels right for my family and in my opinion is worth the up-charge.

Many of the farmers that I had the opportunity to meet on my travels are producing food using organic techniques, but have not gone through the lengthy government certification process. That's where the advantage of eating local really shines. By establishing a dialogue with your local food growers and producers, you're cutting through all of the certifications, labels and such. Visit the farms, ask questions, and even help out if you can. If you're interested in finding more organic growers and suppliers, visit the Organic Consumers Association at www.organicconsumers.org, or if you're one of my Georgia neighbors, visit the Georgia Organics Web site at www.georgiaorganics.org. No matter where you live, you may be surprised how strong the organic movement is and quality organic produce may be as close as your local farmers' market.

Transitional

Making the switch from conventional farming to organic farming is not an easy one for many commercial farmers. For some, the expense is just too high or, depending on their specific crop, there may not be a practical way of producing a profitable crop without the occasional use of chemical supplements or controls. As I write this, there are NO commercial organic peach orchards in the Peach State. There are simply too many pests and diseases that attack the peach trees in our climate. There is a growing movement among conventional farmers to make the transition to organic farming methods and they work closely with their local county extension agents on ways to best bring about that change. I was fortunate to meet with several extension agents around the state. These are people who understand each region's specific pest and disease issues and initiate appropriate research projects to best understand and react to those challenges. So supporting farmers in that transitional phase can help bring about that sometimes costly conversion from conventional to organic farming.

I must admit that my gung ho organic mentality was tempered during my travels around the state of Georgia while working on the production of the *Hans Cooks the South* series for Georgia Public Broadcasting. Farming is hard work and there are so many elements conspiring against each year's crop that it's miraculous that anything ever reaches the market. I met a couple in South Georgia that described their family farm as "almost organic." They set out to be an organic farm, but when it came down to losing their entire crop to an abnormal insect infestation or spraying their plants once, they chose to save their crop and, subsequently, their livelihood. I can't say that I blame them.

I think that a lot of consumers are transitional eaters, and that's not a bad place to be. You buy organic when you can, but you don't lament or fret when the produce you want is not available as organic. The more we support our local farmers, both organic and transitional, the better our local food supply will become.

The World's Best Onion

Oh my. If you've never experienced the wonder that is the Vidalia onion, you're probably curious as to how anyone could get excited about an onion. Truth be told, I get excited about a good many ingredients, but these things are extra special indeed. It seems the sandy, somewhat rocky soil in and around Vidalia is blessed with a naturally low sulfur content which keeps the onions from developing that stinging, almost hot quality most onions possess. Vidalia onions contain a higher natural sugar content than most apples and you truly can pick one up and eat it just like an apple. Some of you may remember my face on the Food Network when I took a bite of what was SUPPOSED to be a Vidalia onion, but in fact was an onion cast from the bowels of Hades. It was by far the hottest damned onion I've ever eaten. I should've been wary of a Vidalia in January, but I'm not always known for my quick intellect.

Of course you can make any of the following recipes with non-Vidalias, but you may have to cut back on the quantity a bit, especially if you're using harsh, winter onions.

Rustic Roasted Garlic Pancake

This is an oven-baked pancake that can makes for an amazing appetizer or as the base for something heartier. Don't be surprised to see the pancake rising like a thing possessed in the oven ... that's part of the fun! I've never had two turn out looking the same, but they're always delicious.

6 cloves roasted garlic
4 eggs
¼ teaspoon grated nutmeg
salt & white pepper
⅔ cup whole what, all-purpose flour
⅔ cup milk
3 tablespoon butter, cut into chips

Mash garlic with a little sea salt until if forms a nice, smooth paste. Whisk with eggs in a large bowl and add the garlic, grated nutmeg, a pinch of salt and white pepper. Then whisk in the flour, adding gradually to avoid lumps. Then whisk in the milk. Pour the resulting batter into a large, buttered, oven proof skillet and dot the butter chips to top. Bake at 450° F for 15 minutes, then reduce the temperature to 350° F and bake for and additional 10 minutes. Tear or slice a piece off of the pancake, spoon a little Vidalia Onion Marmalade on it and see what you think. I bet you won't stop at one piece ...

Vidalia Onion Marmalade

There's nothing like an onion jam or marmalade, and when you're using a sweet Vidalia, the whole thing just comes together beautifully. I serve it with Rustic Roasted Garlic Pancakes, but it also makes a great topping for steaks, seafood, or even pizza.

6 Vidalia onions, sliced
1 tablespoon olive oil
1 teaspoon coriander, ground
1 teaspoon cumin, ground
salt & pepper
1 cup vinegar (cider or white balsamic work well here, but most varieties would work fine)
1 ½ cups light brown sugar

In a large, wide, heavy skillet over medium heat, toast the cumin and coriander for a just about a minute. Then add your oil, onions, salt and pepper and sauté for about 3 minutes or until the onions start to get a little translucent. Add the vinegar and sugar and continue to cook for about 8-10 minutes, stirring frequently. You want much of the liquid to dissipate and the onions to be nice and soft. Remove from the heat and refrigerate. The marmalade will stay in the refrigerator for about a month or more, well covered.

French Onion Soup

I probably polished off a bowl of French Onion Soup every night of my life between the ages of 14 and 17. That's not hard to do when you live above a restaurant! Nearly every time I order one in another restaurant, however, I'm sorely disappointed. It's such an easy soup to make, but apparently it's an easy one to mess up as well. This version is just a little different from the one at the Woodbridge Inn, but only to make it easier for you to prepare at home. You can use just Swiss cheese, but the three-cheese combination is hard to beat.

1 tablespoon olive oil
4-5 Vidalia onions, sliced
salt
1 teaspoon coriander, ground
1 tablespoon Braggs liquid amino acids or low sodium soy sauce
4 cups chicken stock
1 tablespoon red wine
Day old bread, toasted
½ cup Swiss cheese, grated
½ cup mozzarella cheese, grated
½ cup cheddar cheese, grated

In a large, heavy pot on medium-high heat, add the oil, onions, salt, coriander, wine, and Braggs and sauté for about 8 - 10 minutes. You want to the onions to take on just a little color, but not go too brown. Add the chicken stock and bring to a boil. Reduce the heat to a simmer and adjust the soup for seasoning.

To make the cheese caps for the soup, combine the three cheeses and use your fingers to form cheese disc slightly larger than your serving bowl. Smash the cheese disc on top of a small circle of bread and really squish the two together.

To serve: Place soup in a bowl. Lay cheese/bread cap gently on top. Broil for about 4 - 5 minutes or until the cheese is just all gooey and running down the sides of the bowl. It's not a good onion soup if you can't pick the cheese from the side of the bowl with your fingers.

Poke Salad with Dr. Sams

There's no finer example of a Southern gentleman than Dr. Ferrol Sams. If you don't know who he is, I implore you to find out and read his books. His first novel Run with the Horseman is one of those novels that will become a part of your life, his memories become yours. He and his beautiful and fully charming wife Dr. Helen Sams were kind enough to let us take over their kitchen and invade their sanctuary with our cameras, lights, cables and cords during the production of one of the World's Greatest Onion episode of *Hans Cooks the South*. It would be an act of heresy to do a show about Georgia and not include Dr. Sams.

Dr. Sams is one of the few "old-timers" around who still enjoys the pleasures of the native pokeweed. Pokeweed pops up in the spring and people have been eating its tender leaves and stalks since colonial times. The weed has a reputation for being toxic, but if you prepare it correctly it's a remarkable spring treat. Dr. Sams spent hours preparing the greens, boiling and rinsing the leaves and tender peeled stalks twice before finally cooking them one final time. Pokeweed can be an intestinal irritant for some, so if you've never tried it, find an expert like Dr. Sams and let them prepare it for you the first time.

It's quite possible that no one on planet Earth enjoys fresh calves liver as much as Ferrol and Helen Sams and that dish was the real focus of our visit. Liver is one of those things that people either love or hate. It's usually less of a taste issue and more of a texture issue, and I admit, the texture is odd. I love it, but don't eat it too often. For my special lunch with the Sams family, I added dandelion greens for a nice hint of bitter, and a splash of apple cider vinegar for a little twang of sour. My dad likes to eat liver raw with a bit of sea salt and coarse ground pepper. I've tried it that way, but that's when the texture gets a bit too unique for me.

It was a pleasure to cook for the Doctors Sams and I think it was a fitting way to end that particular show. It was one of those days I'll remember until I stop remembering.

Liver & Onions
with Seared Dandelion Greens

2 - 3 pieces bacon, roughly chopped
2 Vidalia onions, chopped
1 bunch dandelion greens, roughly chopped
1 tablespoon butter
1 tablespoon olive oil
2 cups flour
salt & pepper
6-8 oz. extremely fresh calves liver
1 tablespoon apple cider vinegar

Place bacon in a hot, heavy skillet and cook for a minute or two over medium-high heat. Add the onions and bring to sauté.

While onions are sautéing, heat another heavy skillet over medium-high heat and add the butter and oil. Place the flour in a shallow dish and season with the salt & pepper. Coat the liver lightly in flour and place in skillet. Give the pan a good shake to make sure nothing sticks. Cook about 2 - 3 minutes per side, turning only once the first side is nice and crunchy. Liver can be cooked to temperature, so anything from medium-rare up to well done is fine depending on how you like it.

Add dandelion leaves to onion mixture and sauté for about a minute, or until the greens are just wilted. Add the vinegar to the onion mixture, then serve on top of the liver. Serve with some crisp apples and, as Dr. Sams suggests, a cold glass of buttermilk.

For Red Sauce: In a bowl mix ketchup, onions, a splash of water, and half the shrimp together. Add a splash of hot sauce if desired.

For Green Sauce: Grill the tomatillos and the jalapeno for about 2-3 minutes, turning frequently. You want the tomatillos to get a little soft and squishy. In a food processor, pulse the tomatillos, garlic, and jalapeno together until they're thoroughly pureed. Add the lime juice and the cilantro and blend for another 10 seconds or so. Remove from the processor and add the remaining shrimp.

Keep everything nice and chilled until you're ready to assemble the parfaits. When you're ready to serve, simply alternate layers of the green and red cocktails. Feel free to add embellishments like sour cream, more diced onions or tortilla chips.

Garlic

You know how Homer Simpson gets about donuts? Well I'm the same way about garlic. One whiff of the stuff and I'm all slack-jawed and drooling. I've hosted dozens of cooking classes and television shows and used garlic each and every time. From the wild garlicky ramps that shoot up in the spring to the papery bulbs in the fall, I'm addicted to garlic.

In addition to thwarting vampires (a property of the plant that I've yet to validate), garlic is an amazingly healthy food. It has historically been used to treat and prevent high-blood pressure, heart disease, arthritis, and even cancer. The plant contains a natural antibiotic called allicin which helps protect against fungal and microbial infections. So the next time your loved one informs you that you have garlic breath, you can cleverly retort that you don't have garlic breath, you have healthy breath. The best way to combat garlic breath is to make sure that everyone eats plenty of garlic so you all smell the same.

In the kitchen, garlic is one of the most versatile, and in my mind essential, ingredients you can get. Smash it up in dressings and sauces, mince it for a quick sauté with mushrooms or pop it in the oven and roast it. I like to roast garlic anytime we have the oven on so that I'll always have it on hand to smear on some crunchy bread or blend it into some soft butter as a quick topping for grilled meats or veggies. Roasting garlic mellows the bulb's inherent astringency and yields an earthy complexity that is smooth, earthy and down right delicious. To roast garlic, I simply slice off the very top of the bulb, sprinkle it with a little olive oil (or white truffle oil if I'm feeling extravagant) and sea salt, wrap it in foil, pop it in the oven and bake until it's meltingly soft (about 30 minutes at 400° F degrees). It keeps well covered in the fridge for a few days, but it's hard not to eat the cloves warm straight from the oven.

If you're a gardener, save a little dirt for some garlic this year. You can plant individual cloves in September and harvest beautiful bulbs the following summer. Just leave the papery husk on (which helps to prevent fungus) and plant the cloves (pointy-end up) about an inch deep in loose, rich soil. You can plant store-bought varieties, but you'll find much sturdier bulbs at your local farmers' market and you can get great growing tips from someone who obviously knows how to grow garlic in your area. The plant shoots up beautiful purple spheres of flowers which seem to make my neighborhood bees quite happy. I wonder if bees get garlic breath ...

Roasted Garlic & Tomato Soup
with Garlicky Skillet Croutons

Here's a simple soup recipe that utilizes the properties of both roasted and fresh garlic. I like the paring of garlic's astringency and the acidity of the tomatoes. The bread gives the soup a rich, velvety texture and acts as somewhat of a thickening agent. I top the soup with some quick, garlicky (of course) skillet croutons that act as crunchy little islands of flavor in the soup. Of course, a fat grilled cheese sandwich would be best friends with this soup as well. Enjoy!

For the Soup

3 heads of roasted garlic (discard the papery husk and roots)
1 quart chicken stock
3 cups fire-roasted crushed tomatoes (canned are just fine)
2 cups of rough torn bread (preferably dense, chewy farm bread or sourdough)
1 tablespoon minced fresh garlic
1 tablespoon sea salt
coarse ground pepper to taste

In a large, heavy pot, combine the chicken stock, garlic (both types), and the torn bread. Bring the stock to a slow boil, allowing the bread to become totally saturated. Using an immersion blender (or a food processor), blend the stock until the bread is completely dissolved and the garlic is thoroughly pulverized. Next, add the crushed tomatoes, salt, and pepper. I like to have small chunks of tomato in the soup, but if you prefer it smoother you can add the tomatoes before you blend the soup. Adjust your seasonings and enjoy. The soup will last in the refrigerator for several days and is actually quite good served chilled with a dollop of sour cream.

For the skillet croutons

2 cups bread, cubed (preferably the same bread used in the soup)
1 teaspoon minced garlic
chopped garlic chives or scallions
sea salt
White truffle oil (or high quality olive oil)

In a large skillet over medium heat, add cubed bread, garlic, a sprinkle of sea salt and a drizzle of oil. Toss the bread around in the skillet until they're nice and crunchy on the outside and the garlic has started to caramelize. When you're happy with them, turn off the heat and add your garlic chives or scallions. The heat of the croutons and the pan will help them to release a bit of their volatile oils without overcooking them. Pile them on top of your soup while their still warm and you're good to go. I usually eat about half of them while they're cooking, so you may want to start with a bit more than 2 cups!
onions or tortilla chips.

Farmers' Markets

If the old saying "you are what you eat" is true, then you have to eat local to truly be local. There's no better way to find local produce than taking a trip to your neighborhood farmer's market and we're lucky enough to have several in our area. While it is convenient that we can buy fresh plums from Chile in January at the grocery store, nothing beats the taste of fresh fruit picked at the height of its season and delivered straight to the market. But the farmer's market is more than just fruits and vegetables. Homemade jams and pies, local honey, native and ornamental plants, handmade soap, and even handspun yarn can sometimes be found. Some markets even invite local craftsmen and woodworkers to display their works.

The early bird may get the worm, but if you're looking for fresh corn, tomatoes, okra, or beans, it's a good idea to hit the markets early. Vendors arrive early and many of the most popular produce items disappear not long after the sun rises. If you find yourself not finding what you came for, ask a vendor to set something aside for you for the next week.

And "next week" is what market-goers look forward to the most. As the season progresses, the produce begins to change. A small trickle of beans in June turns into a flood of beans in July. Green tomatoes in early summer are replaced by crimson red trophies as summer's heat intensifies. One week, there may be a lone vendor selling blueberries and the next, they're everywhere! The market's ever-changing diversity begs one to visit and visit often.

Peaches

Though we may not grow the most peaches, Georgia is known across the country as the Peach State. I have amazing memories of eating intoxicatingly sweet, juicy peaches as a kid, but I all but abandoned peaches for years. Every peach I would purchase at the grocery store was rock hard, smelled like cardboard (if it smelled of anything at all), and had next to no flavor. Most grocery store peaches are varieties that were developed to ship well, don't bruise and can sit around for weeks without going soft. That may be great for the grocer, but not for us. The best peaches, real peaches smell like heaven and will bruise if you look at them sideways, but have a flavor you'll simply never forget.

And so I set out to find the peaches of my youth and I ended up near Fort Valley, Ga. in a little community called Zenith at the Pearson family's fifth generation peach and pecan farm. That kind of operation is somewhat common in Europe (though less and less it's sad to say), but it's almost unheard of in this country. When Al Pearson talks about his farm and tells stories of his grandfather, there's a sense of pride there that you can almost feel. They may not be the largest peach orchard in the state, but they're worth seeking out. Al and his wife Mary disagree about what variety is their best peach (Mary prefers the white-meat varieties), but they both know they're lucky to be living in the shadow of some of the world's best peach trees.

Peach Bread Pudding
with warm Lemon Butter Peaches

Bread pudding is one of those foolproof dishes that you can whip up on short notice. It's also a great way to use up blemished or overripe fruits. You can substitute peaches for nearly any other fruit, or combine fruits as you like.

For the pudding:

4-5 cups cubed stale bread (preferably whole wheat)

4 eggs

¼ cup raw sugar

2 cups whole milk

1 teaspoon vanilla extract

1 cup peaches, rough chopped

2 cups peaches, diced

½ teaspoon nutmeg, grated

For the Lemon Butter Peaches:

½ stick unsalted butter

¼ cup raw sugar

zest from 1 lemon

juice from ½ a lemon

2 peaches, sliced

1 tablespoon amaretto

2 scoops ice cream

mint to garnish

Preheat your oven to 325° F. Place the bread in a large bowl. Now in a separate bowl, whisk the eggs with the sugar until it's fully combined, then whisk in the milk and vanilla. Pour over bread and let it soak.

In a food processor or blender, puree the chopped peaches. Add the pureed peaches to the bread mixture and stir to combine.

Add the bread mixture to a buttered, ovenproof dish. Scatter the diced peaches over the top and gently swirl in to the pudding. Grate the nutmeg over the top and bake for 40-50 minutes, or until a toothpick inserted into the center comes out clean.

For the Lemon Butter Peaches: Place the butter in a medium skillet over medium-high heat. When butter melts, add the sugar, lemon zest and juice, sliced peaches, and amaretto. Cook until sugar is just melted and peaches are warmed through. If you're cooking over a gas burner, you can make a little show of flaming the whole concoction with a splash of brandy of peach schnapps.

To serve, spoon some bread pudding into individual serving bowls, top with some good vanilla or peach ice cream, then spoon over the warm Lemon Butter Peaches. Garnish with a sprig of mint and get ready for people to ask for seconds.

Peach Quesadilla
with Brie & Peach-Tomato Salsa

Peaches and fennel are a combination you should really see used more often, as each gives a little something to the other. You can spike the salsa with some fresh chilies if you like things a little spicy. You can substitute the chicken thighs with chicken breast if you like, or use shrimp, pork, or even firm tofu.

3 boneless, skinless chicken thighs
1 teaspoon cinnamon
salt & pepper
1 teaspoon avocado oil
1 fennel bulb, sliced into rings (fronds reserved for salsa)
whole wheat tortillas
4-6 oz. Brie cheese, room temperature

For Salsa:

½ Vidalia onion, diced
2 peaches, chopped
1 heirloom tomato
3 tablespoons peach puree or peach butter
1 tablespoon fennel fronds, chopped
salt
avocado or olive oil

For the Salsa:
Mix together onions, peaches, & tomatoes in a bowl with just a pinch of salt. Add the fennel fronds, peach puree, and a just a splash of avocado oil. Cover and refrigerate until you're ready with the quesadillas.

For the quesadillas:
Score the chicken thighs on both sides, being careful not to cut all the way through. Place in a bowl and add the cinnamon, a little pepper, salt, and oil. Mix it all together and then add the chicken to a large grill pan over medium-high heat. When the chicken starts to get some good color, flip the chicken and add the fennel rings to the pan and cook for an additional 3-4 minutes. Make sure your chicken is cooked all the way through, then remove from the heat and cut into strips.

Now, to assemble the quesadillas, place a tortilla on a hot griddle or pan. Place 3 slices of Brie on the tortilla, add some fennel, some chicken, and the top with another slice of Brie to hold it all together. Cover with the other tortilla and let the whole thing go for a few minutes. When one side looks done, flip the quesadilla and cook until the cheese is nice and squishy. When you're ready to serve, slice into four triangles and serve with loads of the fresh Peach –Tomato salsa.

The Sun Always Shines on TV

In the days before there were 5000 channels on television, the only time a kid could catch cartoons was Saturday mornings. For some reason, the good cartoons came on early and the quality of each proceeding program progressively tumbled downhill as noon approached. At some point in the late morning haze of lackluster cartoons, my boredom found me turning the dial (yes, I turned the dial!) through all eleven channels and stopped for no reason at all on PBS. There, in the middle of our console television, stood a silly Chinese man whose bad puns rivaled my father's, but unlike my father, he was having fun. Not that my dad doesn't love to cook, but in my early years, he was always a bit pissed-off in the kitchen, working like a man possessed to throw out 100-plus meals from the Inn's tiny kitchen. But here was this Yan Can Cook guy chopping vegetables in a blur, flipping odd ingredients in an even odder pan (I'd never seen a wok before!), and having a blast! I wanted more.

After my first morning with Yan, Saturdays found me watching Justin Wilson, Jacques Pepin, Julia Childs, and Graham Kerr. Better food was being doled in our restraunt's dining room directly below that television, but these smiley TV cooks were like magicians, popping a cold casserole in one oven then miraculously pulling out the same dish moments later, its molten cheese bubbling like magma. So I watched cooking shows and lived above a restaurant, but I didn't actually start cooking until I was 18 years old and my father was put on dialysis. His kidneys were failing and there was talk that he may not survive. In a snap, my focus turned to the kitchen and I began my apprenticeship in the shadow of Dad's IV pole. After my first night on the line, he told my mother that I didn't have a chance. He's since changed his tune.

In 2004, our local cable company offered me a chance to produce my own cooking show after having appeared as a guest a few times on another show they produced called Flavors of the South. The pilot for In the Kitchen with Hans (obvious name I suppose) played well, but it was a ball of confusion for me. No one gave me any instruction about which camera to talk to, what time cues look like, how long the segments were to be, and so on. As I put the finishing touches on my first dish, one of the crew members held up her finger and waved it in the air like it was on fire. I didn't know if her waving finger meant that I should wait, hurry up, or check the contents of my nostrils. I had to finally stop and just say "What??? Am I doing something wrong?" It turns out the finger meant that I had one minute left before going to break ... who knew?

After nine shows, the station offered me a full-time job, but NOT as a cooking show host. They hired me to be the host of a new local news show called North Georgia Now, which would air every night, Monday through Friday at 7:30. I enjoyed the show tremendously, but it was not the same as being in the kitchen. During the first or second month of being the anchor of that show, my wife Amy received an email about a contest that Food Network was conducting. It was a nationwide search for a new cooking show host in the guise of a reality show: The Next Food Network Star. She called me at work and said simply, "You should enter that. I think you'd win." So, simple as that, I called my friend Brad to come up from Atlanta, have a few beers, and tape what would be my entry video. It was essentially me running my mouth in the Inn's tiny kitchen while putting together a spicy dish of monkfish, okra, and Soloman Gundy ... no cuts, no edits. I submitted the tape and quickly forgot about the whole thing. Out of sight, out of mind.

Fast forward a few months and the phone rings late one Friday. A lady with a thick, Yankee accent (we Southerners can detect that accent after hearing only one syllable) was telling me that my submission video was on the Internet and that I'd already received over 600 votes to be a contestant on The Next Food Network Star. She spoke so quickly that it took my brain a moment to fully comprehend what she was saying. The weeks that followed were a blur. Somehow, Round One ended with me coming out ahead. When the final round of voting began, I had no idea who the thousands upon thousands of people were that were diligently sitting at their computers and casting their votes for me. I had radio stations and news papers phoning, and even received a mysterious call from someone who had been voting for someone else and was now "throwing their weight" behind me. Before I even had time to take it all in, the voting was over and I was going to Manhattan to appear on the Food Network.

Reality television, it turns out, has very little in common with actual reality and after two stressfully fun weeks, I finished third in that competition. I finished third, I was later informed, because I didn't represent the demographic the show was trying to attract. The show went to a well-deserving couple that quickly became life long friends of mine, Dan Smith and Steve McDonough. If you're ever in Chicago, drop in and say "howdy" to the Hearty Boys.

I've worked on two other television series since my cancer battles in 2005 and we've taped over 50 shows. My most recent show, *Hans Cooks the South*, was taped in 2008 and we had the opportunity to tell the story of Georgia's amazing culinary resources. We shot 13 shows in high definition (I've been told I'm too skinny for wide-screen television!) for Georgia Public Broadcasting, but we barely scratched the surface on what this state has to offer. I'd love to do a similar series on Germany to showcase that country's rich culinary treasures to an American audience. I'm not sure what my next television adventure will be, but I know it will truly be an adventure. My favorite thing about cooking is that you simply never stop learning and I love sharing those culinary discoveries with others.

Behind the scenes

I've been blessed to work with some truly talented people on all of my television shows. From the technical to the aesthetic, a great deal of planning and hard work goes into each half hour episode. The sad thing is that most people will never get to experience the zaniness that happens when the cameras are off. When I returned from the hospital and my friend/producer Huitt and I began talking about doing a new series of television shows, my main request was that we just have fun. If it ever stops being fun, I don't want to do it anymore. I'm proud to say that our "have fun" creed has carried us through all sorts of technical difficulties and mishaps with smiles on our faces (thanks in part to a few well-placed "that's what she said" jokes). I've learned a lot from my crew, and hopefully they've learned a few things from me. They're always willing to try my often-strange food experiments and now enjoy everything from squid to kohlrabi. My friend Joe McCutchen once told me that if you surround yourself with successful, positive people, you'll find yourself becoming successful and positive. If it's true that you are who your friends are, then I'm in pretty good shape.

Tomatoes

Scientifically it's a fruit (or a berry if you really want to get technical), but as a commodity it's a vegetable. The very nature of the fruit/vegetable confusion illustrates the versatility of this amazing garden gem. I visited the garden of heirloom tomato aficionado/fanatic Bill Yoder, a man whose knowledge of tomatoes borders on the encyclopedic. Bill and his family grow about 250 varieties of historic heirloom varieties and are part of an international seed exchange program that ensures the future of these seldom seen tomato breeds. While many of these varieties were once hugely popular and readily available in seed catalogs, they didn't quite make the cut when it comes to either ship-ability or long-term storage and are therefore rarely seen in mass markets.

There is really no comparison between these vibrant, sweet, acidic heirlooms and their over-bred, often gassed, industrial counterparts. And nothing rivals a thick-sliced tomato sandwich lathered with mayonnaise and a slice of Vidalia onion. When tomato season hits, wake up early and head to your local farmer's market and see if you can find someone growing some heirloom varieties.

We grow a handful of plants in our backyard each year, most of which end up looking rather pithy thanks to Georgia's fickle supply of rain. Our back patio and deck house a motley collection "self-watering" containers and we invariably have few tomato plants in them. The conditions aren't perfect, but when things get going, we'll average about 4 or 5 tomatoes a day and we always hurry to eat them before the fruit flies in the neighborhood find out about them. Our fruit flies have great taste in tomatoes.

My hunt for tomatoes in the Atlanta area led me to the fine folks at Oakhurst gardens. Oakhurst is a really groovy community garden in Decatur and its heart is larger than its actual square footage. Locals can lease garden plots, but it's really about much more than that. There's a sense of community here that you don't find

in many places, and it's the garden that glues it all together. One of the garden's community projects is the All Girls Green Team and you've never met a more enthusiastic group of young gardeners. Many of them came to the garden with no previous farming experience and a couple of them had never eaten a cherry tomato before that morning. But that didn't take away from their excitement, each of them scurrying from plant to plant like they were looking for diamonds or opals.

The girls take their harvest to local markets twice a week and they get to keep a portion of the proceeds. But I get the feeling that the money isn't the motivation here. These girls have discovered the thrill of the garden and it's something that will stay with them through old age. And hopefully it's something they can pass on to their children and their children to come.

Yellow Tomato & Yellow Watermelon Salad

This is a great way to highlight the fruity side of tomatoes. You can use any color tomato you like, but I like pairing the low-acid yellow varieties with the watermelon, plus the tone on tone theme makes for a beautiful presentation.

3 cups yellow heirloom tomatoes,
cored and rough chopped
½ of a jicama, peeled and diced
¼ cup lettuce leaf basil, chopped
3 cups yellow watermelon, cubed
salt
1 teaspoon cayenne pepper
½ a lime, juiced

This is pretty straightforward. Just mix all of the ingredients together and chill. This is one of those things that gets better after it sits for at least a half hour in the refrigerator.

Yellow Tomato & Yellow Watermelon Gazpacho

If you have any leftover Tomato & Watermelon salad, why not pulse it into a smooth and refreshing gazpacho?

3 cups Yellow Tomato & Yellow Watermelon salad
1 tablespoon avocado or olive oil
1 teaspoon white balsamic vinegar
dollop of sour cream
cayenne pepper, for garnish

Put the salad in a food processor and add the oil and vinegar. Blend together until you reach the desired consistency. I like to get it smooth, but with some little chunks still in there for some texture. Serve in a chilled bowl or glass and top with sour cream and a dash of cayenne pepper.

Variation – Green Gazpacho
To make this verde version, simply substitute honeydew melon for the watermelon and use "ripe when green" heirloom tomatoes. A little fresh pressed parsley or spinach juice will add a nice green punch as well.

Open-Faced Tomato Sandwich with a Sun-dried Tomato & Caper Tapenade Mayo

This sandwich was inspired by one my father used to make for us on cold days at the Inn. His version utilized 1000 Island dressing and bacon, but the overall feel of a warm, cheesy, tomato sandwich is the same. This recipe makes way more Tapenade Mayo than you'll need, but it keeps well and you'll find yourself using it on other sandwiches.

For the Tapenade Mayo:

1 cup sun-dried tomatoes
2 cloves garlic
2 tablespoons capers
½ Vidalia onion
1 tablespoon avocado oil
2 cups mayonnaise (store bought or homemade)

Blend the first 5 ingredients (all but the mayo) in a food processor until homogenous, but somewhat chunky. Mix in the mayonnaise and set aside while you work on the sandwiches.

For Sandwiches:

2 slices of good bread (something dark or nutty works well here)
sliced Vidalia onions
tomatoes, sliced
salt
4 slices Munster cheese
lovage leaves

Place the bread onto a sheet pan and turn on your oven's broiler. Generously spread the Tapenade Mayo on the two pieces of bread. Add the sliced Vidalia onions and the sliced tomatoes and sprinkle with sea salt. Add two slices of cheese to each sandwich. Place under the broiler (not too close to the heating element) and let it cook for 3-4 minutes or until the cheese is bubbly and just starting to brown. Garnish with chopped lovage and enjoy!

Cherry Tomato Curry

I'm a sucker for a good curry. My sister Sonja and I shared a place during our university years and we lived right across the street from a good Indian restaurant. I used to go and sit there for hours reading Clive Barker novels and stuffing myself with curry and crispy onion naan. This dish was inspired by my favorite Indian restaurant, a great little vegetarian place in Marietta, Ga. called Vatica. The owner, a jovial man that reminds me a bit of my father, claims that what they serve at the restaurant is simply "peasant food". If that's the truth, then I simply adore peasant food. The chickpeas add enough protein to make this a perfect vegetarian meal.

2 tablespoon avocado oil
1 teaspoon mustard seed
1 teaspoon coriander
1 teaspoon turmeric
1 teaspoon cumin
1 teaspoon freshly grated ginger root
1 ½ Vidalia onion, thinly sliced
2 cloves garlic, sliced
1 bunch cilantro
2 teaspoon double concentrated tomato paste
1 pint cherry tomatoes
2 cans fire roasted crushed tomatoes
juice from ½ a lime
2 cans chick peas, drained & rinsed
cooked basmati rice
dollop of plain yogurt

Heat a large skillet on medium heat and add the oil, mustard, coriander, turmeric, cumin, and ginger. Fry the spices for about 30 seconds then add the onion and garlic. Cut the stems off the cilantro, finely chop them and then add them to the skillet. Sauté for 2 - 3 minutes until the onion becomes soft and translucent. Add the tomato paste, cherry tomatoes, crushed tomatoes, lime juice and chickpeas. Bring the curry to a low boil, then reduce heat and simmer for 6-8 minutes. Right before service, rough chop the cilantro leaves and stir them into the curry. Serve over basmati rice with a dollop of plain yogurt and a bit more fresh cilantro to garnish.

There's No Such Thing as Stale Bread

One of the few foods that is common in almost all cultures is bread ... and for good reason. Nothing can rival the smell of bread baking, be it foccaccia, naan, bagels, or a golden, flaky baguette. Bread has been around for centuries and its preparation is an intrinsic part of daily life in most countries. Bread is a symbol of fecundity, prosperity, and of life itself.

Bread is a living thing, and it's born the moment that the yeast is hydrated. Yeast thrives in the warm, moist mix and feeds on the sugars in the flour. As the yeast respires, air is trapped in the dough and, as if by magic, the living mass rises. The oven marks the end of the yeasts' life, but it's the fulcrum moment for the bread ... too little heat and the bread turns dense and hard, too much and the crust turns brittle and dark. But if the conditions are just right, the spongy dough sets and the crust turns ... well, crusty. Perfection! Anyone not truly fascinated by bread is sleeping their way through life.

What a tragedy it is if, after all of the baker's toils, a half-eaten loaf of bread ends its life in the bottom of the trash bin. In every culture there are recipes for stale bread to spare the baker from such woes. Day-old, or even week-old bread becomes an entirely new ingredient with its own unique properties and uses in the kitchen. It can be grated into breadcrumbs to coat a cutlet, sliced and soaked in eggs to make French toast, or cubed and tossed in olive oil and herbs to make some savory croutons. Bagel makers discovered that if they thinly sliced and baked their day-old products, the resulting chips would be as popular as fresh bagels. If it's true that necessity is the mother of invention, I think that it must also be true that a good cook is necessity's other child.

Bread pudding is one of my favorite ways to resurrect otherwise doomed bread. Typically, bread pudding is a sweet concoction full of rum-soaked raisins, cinnamon, sugar, and perhaps a banana or apple thrown in for good measure. Sweet bread puddings are my weakness and I used to haunt a place in Midtown Atlanta who, at one time, had the best bread pudding with whiskey sauce in the Southeast (sadly, they no longer serve bread pudding). I made an Peach Bread Pudding with some amazing Georgia peaches on *Hans Cooks the South*.

Zucchini and Sun-Dried Tomato Bread Puddings

Bread pudding doesn't necessarily have to be sweet. For this recipe, I combined grated zucchini and sun-dried tomatoes to make a savory variety. It works as a delicious alternative to Yorkshire pudding for your prime rib or as a great side with fried chicken. Because no two breads are created equal, you may have to increase or decrease the amount of milk in the recipe, depending on how much your bread absorbs. You want the mixture to be well moistened, but not overly soggy. Enjoy!

½ cup sun-dried tomatoes, chopped
6 cups of stale bread, cubed
(I used a good 9-grain here)
1 cup zucchini, grated
1 cup whole milk
3 eggs
2 cloves garlic, minced
1 teaspoon salt
½ cup grated cheese (your choice, but a
firm Swiss would work well here)

In a large bowl, whisk together eggs, milk, garlic, and salt. Stir in the bread, zucchini, cheese (if you're so inclined), and the sun-dried tomatoes and let the whole mixture soak for about 20 minutes. Pour into a baking dish or greased muffin pan and bake in a preheated 350° F oven for 20-25 minutes, or until a knife inserted comes out clean. Bread pudding is fairly foolproof, so feel free to experiment with your own favorite ingredients.

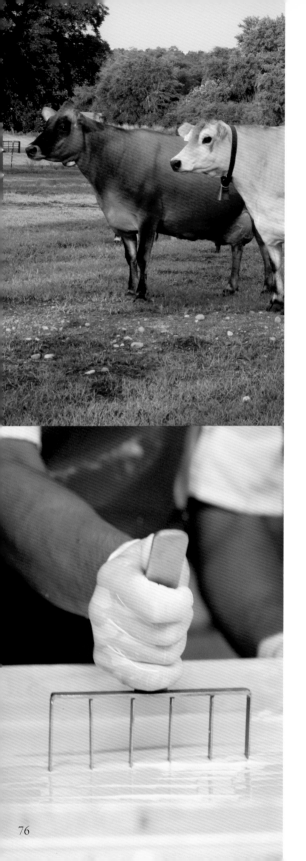

Cheese

There's something downright magic about the cheese-making process. The very notion that you can transform something as liquid as milk into something as complex and intricate as cheese is simply remarkable. You can taste the amount of time and energy that goes into each handcrafted batch of cheese. And once the curds have been separated from the whey, a complex mingling of time, temperature, and humidity (and perhaps a bit of luck) works to mature the cheese to its full potential. I grew up within sniffing distance of my father's breakfast Limburger, cautiously learning to love its bracing first notes right through to its buttery smooth finish. From that point forward I've embraced cheese with on open mind and an open mouth. From strong and upfront to mellow and reserved, from hard as bricks to soft as silk, there's a cheese out there for everyone.

The hunt for local cheeses led me to the town of Swainsboro, Ga. and a hunting/fishing/farming property called Flat Creek Lodge. Sprawling over 2000 acres (200 of which are ponds and lakes), Flat Creek jumped into the cheese making business head first, importing cheesemakers from the Cheese Head state of Wisconsin. The farm is producing some amazing varieties from farmhouse to cheddars, blues to proprietary cheeses like Thai Basil and Aztec with cocoa and peppers. My favorite was a semi-soft variety called Gnupa, which I suppose you would classify as a "stinky" cheese. Delicious. Flat Creek's cheeses are starting to find their way into some of the State's better gourmet shops and eateries and if they're not in your area yet, ask for them. They're truly worth seeking out.

My cheese adventure then led me down to southwest Georgia to the thriving little town of Thomasville. Not only did we get to sample some of the award-winning cheeses at Sweet Grass Dairy, we also sampled even more cheese at a fun little restaurant downtown called Liam's. And when lunch was over, we went back to the dairy and ate even more cheese. There's very little you can complain about when you have that much cheese on the agenda.

The folks at Sweet Grass know their craft and are constantly pushing themselves to improve their already brilliant cheeses.

No matter where you live, I guarantee there's someone making cheese near you. So the next time you go out shopping for cheese, put down that waxy, plasticky stuff and seek out one of your local cheeses. You'll thank me for it.

Pear & Three Cheese Pizza

Pizza is the perfect canvas for introducing flavors to people who might otherwise be afraid to try new things. I've turned many folks on to goat cheese by sneaking it on to a pizza ... nefarious, I realize, but effective. In this preparation I used an aged goat cheese called Holly Springs from Sweet Grass Dairy, and a trappist style, triple-cream cheese from Flat Creek Lodge called Gnupa. But feel free to experiment with your favorite cheeses or be adventurous and try some new cheeses from your local purveyor. I love using the Indian-style flatbread called naan, which you can find in many of the larger markets these days, but you can use any prepared pizza crust if you like.

2 pears, cored, peeled, and chopped
½ cup Holly Springs cheese, cubed
½ Gnupa cheese, cubed
1 tablespoon pear infused vinegar
2 tablespoons olive oil
salt
pepper
2 pieces of naan flatbread or pita
2 tablespoons chevre cheese
4 slices of salami, cut into slivers
fresh thyme

Preheat the oven to 450° F.

In a large bowl, toss together the first 5 ingredients and season with a little salt and pepper. Spread the each piece of naan with 1 tablespoon of chevre, then divide the pear/cheese mixture between the two pizzas. Sprinkle the top of each with the salami and fresh thyme leaves. Bake in the oven for about 10 minutes or until the cheese has turned nice and bubbly. Garnish with more thyme and eat it while it's hot. I like to serve this with a little mixed salad right on top of the pizza and eat the whole thing with a knife and fork. Good stuff!

Monte Cristo Sandwich

A Monte Cristo is essentially two pieces of French Toast with ham, cheese, and some good jam in between. You rarely see Monte Cristo sandwiches on menus these days, but there was a time when they were a standard, and I miss them. Most places served them under a thick dusting of powdered sugar, but I think that's overkill. A good spoonful of homemade preserves is all the sweet you need. I also like using pflaumenmuss, a German plum butter (similar to apple butter) that you can find in specialty shops. You can use a good Swiss cheese for your sandwich, but the herbal notes of the Leyden cheese make it worth seeking out.

4 slices of Leyden cheese, thinly sliced
plum jam
1 tablespoon butter
1 tablespoon olive oil
¼ cup milk
3 eggs
2 slices whole wheat bread
4-5 thin slices Black Forest-style ham

Whisk the eggs and milk together in a shallow bowl. Heat the butter and oil in a large skillet over a medium-high heat. Dip both sides of the bread in the egg mixture, letting the bread absorb the mixture. Cook the bread in the skillet for about 2-3 minutes per side, flipping once the first side is golden brown. If it seems at this point like you're making French Toast, it's because you ARE making French Toast! As soon as you make that first flip, spread some plum jam on the bread, then pile on some cheese, ham, more cheese, and then cover with the other piece of bread. Flip the sandwich one last time continue for just another minute until the cheese is all runny. This is meant to be a messy sandwich! Cut the sandwich diagonally and serve with a little more jam on the side.

"The more I do learn about cheese, the more I know nothing." - Dane Huebrer (Flat Creek Lodge)

Restaurant Boy

I am a restaurant boy. Every childhood memory I have took place in a restaurant, above a restaurant, on the way to a restaurant or returning from a restaurant. Those memories, either good or bad, are forever linked to not only the restaurants, but to the food itself, be it bad or good. So I guess I'm not just a restaurant boy… I'm a food boy. Food has defined me. Some people have soundtracks to their lives and some have screenplays … I have a menu. Every smell and texture and taste evokes a strong connection with the first or worst or best experience I had with that food. When I eat gravlax, it's 1982 and I'm with my Uncle Wolfgang in Trondheim, Norway; banana pudding or fried okra and I'm back in my grandmother's kitchen in Atlanta. These collected eating experiences are the common threads that hold my timeline together.

My family purchased the Woodbridge Inn restaurant in 1976 when I was four years old. The Inn, originally called the Lenning Hotel, was built in the mid-1800's and had once been a popular vacation spot for Floridians wanting to escape the summer heat. It was all but derelict when my parents purchased it. We moved into the upstairs portion where the guests once slept and before we knew it, my sister Sonja and I were restaurant children. Living twelve-and-a-half steps above one of North Georgia's landmark restaurants ensured that our lives would never be boring. It was frustrating, exhausting, exciting and ridiculously stressful all at the same time. If we needed help with our Math homework, we'd take the books to the kitchen and ask Dad questions between pickups. If we wanted a snack we'd go downstairs and order off the menu. If the restaurant got slammed, we'd run down the stairs to work. I've washed dishes and shucked oysters in my pajamas more times than I care to admit.

I was raised in a house of food, and to this day, food permeates my every thought. I plan my day around what I'm going to eat and when. When we go on vacation, I'm more concerned about where we're going to eat than what we're going to do when we get there. I am obsessed with food. My stomach cancer operations left me chewing nothing but ice during my eight-week hospital stay. During that time I would walk with my family and friends to the cafeteria, pushing my IV pole and my collection of drainage tubes and drip-lines, collecting awkward looks from the "healthy" diners in the room. I think people felt guilty consuming food in front of me, but watching others eat gave me great joy and invaluable inspiration. That cafeteria became my surrogate restaurant and those foodless meals were an important part of my recovery. Mealtime is such an integral stitch in my fabric that I simply cannot imagine life without it, even if I'm not the one doing the eating.

81

Herbs

A little bit of dirt and a modest amount of sunshine. That's really all you need to get your own herb garden up and thriving. I know some of you are looking at your thumbs right now to see if they possess any traces of green, but even the most disastrously brown-thumbed, failed gardener can grow herbs as easily as growing weeds. The truth is, many of my favorite herbs become seriously weed-like in just a few short years. Take mint for example. Once you have mint, you'll have it for life, often sprouting in places you'd least expect it. Our modest collection of mint apparently learned a thing or two from our native kudzu and likes to pop up in the lawn (which smells delightful when we mow) and even in containers far away from its original happy hole in the ground. And speaking of containers, most herbs will thrive without a care in any old pot filled with any old dirt. In fact, most herbs prefer poor soils and thrive on neglect. The best part is, they reward you year after year with an amazing source of flavor that adds punch to all manner of foods.

My children can't wait to run into the yard to nibble on things like fresh basil, fennel fronds and seeds, nasturtium blossoms, lemon balm, lemon verbena, and, of course, mint. They're always eager to introduce their friends to these little herb-garden treasures, many of whom rarely eat anything fresh or green at all. Sometimes their friends will wrinkle their noses and pretend that what they're chewing is vile, but later I'll catch them returning to the plants for just one more pinch. So if you have any dirt on your property or even just a patio or deck with some neglected containers, buy some herbs and experience the magic that these unassuming, hardy little plants offer.

Herb Butter

I love making herb butters, and just like the Green Goddess dressing, each batch varies depending on what looks good in the garden. The herb butter can last in the freezer for several months and works well on seafood, meats, potatoes, pasta, and all sorts of grilled vegetables, especially on grilled ears of corn.

4 tablespoons fresh parsley
1 tablespoon fresh sage
2 tablespoons fresh rosemary, stems discarded
2 tablespoons fresh oregano, stems discarded
1 lb. butter, room temperature
1 teaspoon freshly grated nutmeg
1 teaspoon ancho chili powder
½ teaspoon paprika
½ tablespoon sea salt

Rough chop the herbs, or pulse them briefly in a food processor. Combine the chopped herbs with the butter, chili powder, nutmeg, paprika, and salt. Roll the herb butter in parchment paper and freeze. Whenever you're ready for a taste of fresh herbs, just cut off a slice and melt on top of anything you're serving. Try experimenting with other flavors like sun-dried tomatoes, olives, lemon, etc.

Zipper Peas with Fennel

There's nothing like fresh peas and if you hit the market at the right time, you can buy plenty to eat right then and some to freeze for later. And the best part about peas is that you can make all sorts of "pea" jokes with your kids. "Hey Finn, do you mind if I pea on your plate?" "Hey Ella, it looks like someone pea'd in your rice!" Nothing inspires an instant guffaw like well placed potty humor, or in this case, mock-potty humor.

1 medium fennel bulb, roughly chopped
1 tablespoon butter
¼ cup water
2 cups zipper peas, or black eyed peas
2 sprigs mint leaves, chopped fine
salt/pepper

Add the butter, water, fennel, and peas in a heavy, medium sized pot. Cover and cook on a medium-low heat for about 10 - 15 minutes, or until the peas are just tender. Add fresh chopped mint the last minute and adjust seasoning with a little salt and pepper.

Green Goddess Dressing

Green Goddess is an herb lover's dream, and it's never the same thing twice. In my opinion, that's a good thing! If you don't have sorrel or burnet, get some! And if you can't find them, just use any tasty, leafy green herbs at your disposal. Woody herbs like thyme, rosemary and lavender can be a bit strong for this delicate dressing, so try sticking to tender, soft-leaved herbs like oregano, basil, mint, lemon balm, fennel, dill, and the like. I like the thickness of Greek yogurt in this dressing, but if you can't find it, try straining regular plain yogurt through a fine sieve lined with cheesecloth.

1 garlic clove
1 tablespoon burnet leaves
3-4 sorrel leaves, rough chopped
2 tablespoons lemon verbena leaves
2 tablespoons Greek basil leaves
2 tablespoons mint leaves
¼ cup fennel stems and fronds
salt
pepper
6 tablespoons white balsamic vinegar
1 cup Greek yogurt
3 tablespoon avocado oil

Combine all ingredients in a food processor and blend until smooth. Serve with crisp greens like mache, arugula, or even watercress. Green Goddess also makes an excellent dip for raw veggies or even as a spread for sandwiches.

Seared Tuna
with Gremolata

Gremolata is the Italians' answer to pesto. Wait, the Italians do pesto too … so, it's the Italians' other pesto-like, fresh herb sauce. I love the fresh, green taste of parsley and gremolata really showcases that herb's often-overlooked flavor. Most Americans think of parsley as an unwanted green garnish and it usually gets flung to the side. But parsley is loaded with healthy chlorophyll and actually helps keep your breath smelling sparkly. But of course, when you're adding in 4 cloves of garlic, all bets are off. Gremolata works really well with seafood, meats, pasta, and even as a topping for good crunchy bread. Give it a try.

For the Tuna:

2 4-6 oz. tuna steaks
zest from 1 lime
½ teaspoon red chili flakes
½ tablespoon oil
salt

For the Gremolata:

4 garlic cloves
½ cup Vidalia onion, chopped
½ bunch parsley
2 tablespoons chives, roughly chopped
4 tablespoons avocado oil
Juice and pulp from 1 lime

To make the gremolata, pulse together the lime juice and pulp, garlic, onion, parsley, chives, avocado oil, and a good pinch of salt in a food processor or blender until the sauce is slightly chunky, but homogenous.

Put the lime zest, chili flakes, and a little sea salt on a plate. Pat the tuna steaks on the plate, covering each piece with the mixture.
Add the ½ tablespoon of oil to a heavy skillet over medium-high heat. When the oil is hot and wavy, place the tuna steaks in the pan and sear 1-2 minutes per side. Tuna is best eaten rare to medium rare.
To serve, simply plate the fish and spoon loads of gremolata on top. If you have extra limes, serve some extra wedges with the fish. A good splash of fresh lime juice always makes things taste just a little brighter.

The Right Fish

In the late '80's, almost every restaurant worth mentioning had Orange Roughy on its menu. Similar to flounder in both taste and texture, it was a seemingly abundant species that was easy on the palate for the "I don't want fish that tastes like fish" diners. The Orange Roughy lives to be more than 150 years old and only reproduces late in life, which means we were eating all of the potential parents. Today, only 7 percent of their numbers remain. We've almost eaten them all.

The same thing is happening now with the Patagonian Toothfish, or as it's more politely called, the Chilean Sea Bass (sounds better than Toothfish, right?) Using fishing lines more than 60 miles long, fishing vessels have almost wiped out the Toothfish, along with countless other unintended animals like sea turtles and birds. Yet for some reason, you still see Chilean Sea Bass on the menu of many trendy restaurants.

The statistics paint a grim picture that leaves our "bountiful oceans" barren. So what can you do about it? Eat wisely! The Monterey Bay Aquarium compiles a Seafood Watch list that educates consumers on what fish to avoid, and more importantly, which fish and other seafood are fine to eat. You can find that list, and even print out a pocket guide, at: http://www.mbayaq.org/cr/seafoodwatch.asp.

The term aquaculture may be new to some, but essentially it's the seafood equivalent of farming. Like all farming, it's important to seek out and support those farms that are taking all the necessary steps to protect both the quality of both their "crop" and their environment. Early aquaculture practices gave the industry somewhat of a black eye, but luckily those are mostly a thing of the past. As with any food, it's important to know where the food comes from and how it is produced. Establish a relationship with a reputable local fishmonger and don't be afraid to ask questions.

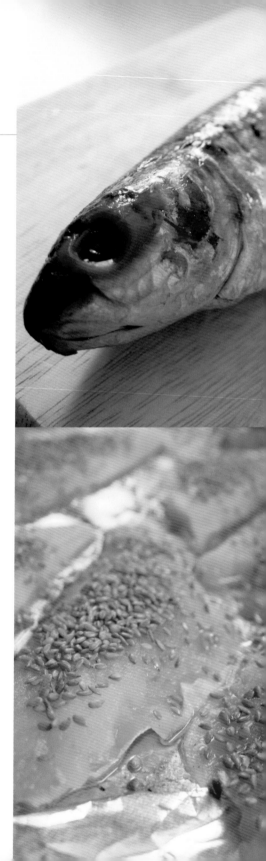

Smoked Trout Cakes with fresh Horseradish Dill sauce

While eel is probably my favorite variety of smoked fish, trout isn't too far behind. Buttery smooth and full of flavor, smoked trout trumps crabmeat in this memorable appetizer. The sauce is tangy-hot yet sweet and pairs nicely with the woody, smokiness of the fish. If you can't find smoked trout, substitute with smoked whitefish or hot-smoked salmon.

For the cakes:

1 whole smoked trout, skin and bones removed
1 whole egg
2 tablespoons mayonnaise (homemade or prepared)
¾ - 1 cup whole wheat bread crumbs
1 tablespoon relish (I like using Vidalia Onion relish, but pickle relish works fine)
1 tablespoon oil
1 tablespoon butter

For the sauce:

1-2 teaspoons fresh grated horseradish root
1 cup crème fraîche or sour cream
2 teaspoons raw sugar
1 tablespoon fresh dill, finely chopped

The flavor of the sauce really develops as it sits, so let's make it first. Simply combine all of the ingredients and refrigerate. The heat of fresh horseradish can really vary, so add as much or as little as you like until you reach your preferred level of "heat".

To make the cakes, crumble the smoked trout into a medium bowl, being extra diligent to remove any of the fine pin-bones. Add the relish, egg, and mayonnaise and stir gently to combine. Add enough breadcrumbs to make the mixture hold together. You don't want it too dry or the cakes will be crumbly. Form small patties with the mixture and set them on a plate sprinkled with a few extra breadcrumbs.

Add the butter and oil to a skillet (I like using cast iron here) over medium-high heat. When the butter has fully melted, sauté the crab cakes until their nice and golden brown, about 2-3 minutes per side. Serve with some crisp greens or sprouts, plus the Horseradish Dill sauce and a sprig of fresh dill to garnish.

Tilapia en Papillote

En Papillote (pronounced on poppy-yot') simply means in parchment and it's a fantastic way to cook fish. Essentially you're making an envelope that traps in all the moisture and flavor of the fish and its accompanying ingredients. If you'd like to include more fish into your diet but are unsure how to begin, try this easy, virtually foolproof cooking technique.

2 6-8oz. fresh tilapia fillets
juice, zest, and pulp from 1 lemon
2 tablespoons sundried tomato and olive tapenade (prepared or homemade)
1 tablespoon roasted pumpkinseed oil
1 ½ cups oyster mushrooms, sliced
2 cloves garlic, sliced
1 cup prepared artichoke hearts, quartered
1 cup cauliflower florets, steamed until tender
¼ cup Vidalia onion, diced
¼ cup red or yellow bell pepper, diced
salt and pepper
parchment paper (NOT wax paper!)
1 ½ cups cous cous

Put the cous cous in a fine-mesh sieve, rinse with cold water and set it aside for a few moments while you prepare the rest. In a medium bowl, mix together the lemon (juice, zest and pulp), tapenade, pumpkinseed oil, mushrooms, artichokes, cauliflower, onion, bell pepper and a little salt and pepper.
Lay a sheet of parchment paper out on a flat surface and brush it with a little melted butter or oil. Place about ¾ cup of the rinsed cous cous in a little pile on the front half of the paper (you'll be folding the paper over in a moment, so don't put things in the exact center). Place a tilapia fillet on top of the cous cous and season the fish with a little salt and pepper. Put about a cup to a cup and a half of the artichoke/mushroom/cauliflower mix on top of the fish and drizzle it all with just a little more pumpkinseed oil. Fold the parchment paper over the fish and seal the package by making small, overlapping folds. Put the parcels on a baking sheet and bake at 350° F for about 8-10 minutes. Remove from the oven and let the packages rest for about 2 minutes before cutting them open to reveal the insides.

One of my first memories of pulling a wriggling fish out of the water is from the Price Creek trout farm that supplied fresh fish to the Woodbridge Inn. I used to sit on a wooden bench next to my father in the tiny kitchen, dredging trout in flour for him to finish off in an old, warped, fire-stained skillet. My dad devised a way to debone the fish using your hands and I mastered the technique at an early age. All feeling left your icy fingers after about 30 fish or so. I can't even begin to imagine how many trout we've sold at the Inn, or subsequently how many I've deboned, but it remains one of my favorite fish to eat. My son Finn now orders trout at the Inn and I must say it makes me tingle with pride every time.

Tilapia is farm raised in nearly every warm country and here in the southern United States. It has firm, snapper-like flesh that will please those "non-fishy" fish eaters. Because its flavor is mild, it lends itself to nearly every cooking style … blacken it in a cast iron skillet, cube it and stir fry it, broil it stuffed with crabmeat, and so on. It's available year round in most markets and it if you buy it frozen, it thaws well with very little change in texture. And if that weren't enough, you can eat Tilapia with a clear conscience, knowing you did your little part in helping to conserve our fragile oceans.

Catfish is another fish that's being successfully aqua cultured with impressive results. Wild-caught catfish can often taste like the waters from which they were harvested, sometimes tasting earthy or just downright muddy. Properly farm-raised fish spend their days in clear, clean, free-flowing water, which gives the fish a mild, sweet flavor that elevates the fish's culinary applications. Exceptionally flaky with no "fish" aftertaste, catfish works well pan-fried, baked, or broiled. If you have bad catfish connotations, give your local farm-raised catfish a chance. You may be pleasantly surprised.

Parmesan Catfish Grenoble

For the fish:

4 catfish fillets (about 4-6 oz. each)
¾ cup freshly grated Parmesan cheese
1 teaspoon smoked paprika
1 tablespoon flat leaf parsley, chopped
3 eggs, beaten
1 cup flour (for dredging)
salt/pepper
butter (for frying)

For the Grenoble topping:

1 large lemon, zested, peeled, seeded, and roughly chopped
2 tablespoons capers, drained
1 sweet onion, diced
1 large tomato, diced
⅓ cup fresh scallion greens, chopped

Season fish fillets with salt and white pepper. In a shallow bowl, combine cheese, paprika, and parsley. Dredge each fillet in flour, then into the beaten eggs, then into the cheese mixture, pressing firmly to make sure the fish is totally covered and as dry as possible. Heat butter over medium flame and fry fillets until golden brown, about 3 minutes on each side. Drain filets on paper towels and either serve immediately or hold in a warm oven until service.

In a small bowl, combine lemon, tomatoes, capers, onions, scallions, and about 1 tablespoon of olive oil. Just before service, heat this mixture on very high heat for just a moment so that the ingredients get hot, but are not cooked. Spoon mixture over fish fillets and garnish with reserved lemon zest.

Figs: The Outside-In Flower

Open my refrigerator and you'll find a veritable museum of half-empty jelly jars, each one with a history and each one preserving the flavors of some season's fecundity. The pantry also sports an impressive collection of preserves, but it's gotten to the point where I'm not allowed to open new jars until I make use of the ones whose tops have been popped. Preserves hold a special place in my collection of culinary treasures and they find their way into salad dressings, marinades, desserts, and barbecue sauce. That sticky sweetness adds not only flavor, but a viscosity and shine that you just can't get with anything else. Each jar of homemade preserves is unique, each one special, but in my haphazard collection, there's none as special as my figs.

Figs have always been special to me. I remember visiting my grandfather in Canon, Ga. where the fried okra and fresh figs impressed me more than his policeman's paraphernalia. I remember him pinching open a fresh fig between his thumbs, revealing the squishy insides that house the intricate parts of its blossom (figs are technically not a fruit, but more of an outside-in flower…but you can call it a fruit). His wife Geneva was (and still is) a master at preserving the bounty of their lone fig tree and I still look forward to her jars of dark, sticky fig jam.

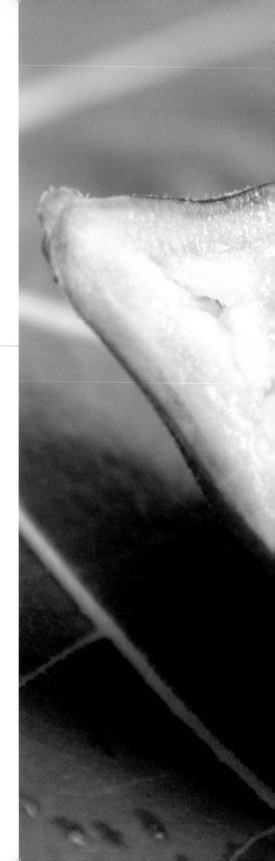

Grilled Quail with Fig-Chipotle BBQ Sauce

I've been making this BBQ sauce for years and it works well on all sorts of foods. Of course my favorite is made with dark, sticky fig preserves, but you can substitute other fruit preserves and marmalades and come up with equally delicious variations. If you like your BBQ sauce on the sweeter side, try adding a good drizzle of sorghum or molasses. If you have fresh figs on hand, try grilling a few along side the quail.

For the Quail:

5-6 boneless quail breasts
1 clove garlic, minced
1-2 teaspoons avocado oil or olive oil

For the Sauce:

1 14.5 oz. can fire-roasted tomatoes (about 2 cups)
1-2 tablespoons chipotles in adobo sauce
2 tablespoons fig preserves
2 tablespoons white balsamic or cider vinegar
½ cup diced Vidalia onion
1-2 cloves of garlic
salt and pepper to taste

First, simply marinate the quail in the oil and garlic. Quail is a very delicate, tender meat that really needs very little in the way of preparation.

To make the sauce, simply pulse all of the ingredients together in food processor. You can adjust the heat of the sauce by adding more chipotle peppers, but start with less and add more as you go. You can always add heat, but it's hard to take it away.

Using a grill or grill pan, simply grill the quail breasts on medium heat for about 2 minutes per side. Once you've made the first flip, brush some of the BBQ sauce on the cooked side and then repeat when the other side is finished. Serve plenty of sauce on the side for dipping. I like to serve this dish with Vidalia Onion Grits and even a little sautéed baby bok choy.

Figs have long been a symbol of fertility and fecundity and the leaves were apparently used to cover Adam and Eve's naughty bits. What more could you ask for? I've seen recipes using the fig leaves much the same way you would use grape leaves in dolmas, but fig leaves have a bit of a funky smell to them. I love foraging in the fig tree for the ripe fruits/flowers, but the leaves always smell a wee bit like cat urine to me. Even the cats look affronted when I'm rustling through the leaves on the hunt for a ripe fig.

The best part about figs is that they're so easy to grow and, lucky for me, they adore Georgia's stifling heat and humidity. Native to the Mediterranean, fig trees only require a bit of lime to feel right at home in your backyard. My sister and I purchased a fig tree for our parents' 30th anniversary and it still stands today, producing 20 to 30 pounds of figs each season. A rogue frost killed the plant to the ground during its third or fourth year, but it bounced back with vigor, new branches racing for the sun each subsequent year until it reached its current height of nearly 40 feet. I have three modest fig trees in my own backyard that were purchased on clearance one fall at a local nursery. They weren't planted to signify any special event or anniversary, but they are a special part of our little yard. The plants are still small, but we treat each ripe blossom like the Queen's jewels, watching them each and every day until they turn ruby red and heavy. On days when we only have one ripe fig, I pinch the fruit in half with my thumbs and share a bit of my history with our two young children. And when Jack Frost strips the leaves from our little trees, we pop open a jar of Geneva's fig preserves and experience the magic one more time

Fig Preserves

No, this isn't Geneva's recipe for fig preserves. In truth, I don't know how she makes them. I'm afraid that if she divulges her secrets, she won't be as compelled to send me those highly-anticipated jars each year. What I need to do is have her write down her methods and send them to me in a double sealed envelope, which I will only open in the event of an emergency!
This recipe yields a fine batch of preserves though, no worries. Eat as many fresh figs as you can possibly handle, then preserve the rest for later. You'll be happy you did.

2 lbs. firm fresh figs
3 ½ cups turbinado sugar
2 ½ cups water
2 tablespoons lime juice
½ teaspoon ground cardamom

First, gently rinse the figs in a colander to remove any dirt or critters. In a heavy, non-reactive pot, place the figs and sugar in alternating layers. Cover and let stand at room temperature overnight.

The next morning, add water to the pot and bring to a gentle boil, cover and let simmer for about 45 minutes over medium heat. The jam is finished when the syrup has thickened enough to coat the back of a spoon. Add cardamom and lime juice, then turn off the heat.

Sterilize jelly jars in boiling water, drain and dry. Fill the jars with hot preserves and seal them. Store the preserves in a cool, dark place and they'll last for a year or more … if you don't eat them first!

Mascarpone Fig Brulee

Easy and delicious. Enough said.

4-5 fig cookies (Fig Newtons or similar)
1 cup mascarpone cheese
2 teaspoons fig jam
1-2 tablespoons local honey
½ teaspoon pure vanilla extract
5-6 fresh figs, sliced
1 teaspoon raw sugar

Pulse the fig cookies in a food processor until they're nice and crumbly. Whisk together the mascarpone cheese, fig preserves, honey, and vanilla extract. If the preserves are super sweet, you can omit the honey or, alternatively, omit the jam and just use the honey. Easy stuff.
Now in a small glass, alternately layer the crushed cookies, sliced figs, and mascarpone mix until the glass is nice and full. Sprinkle a thin layer of raw sugar over the top and, using a small blow torch (available at any hardware department in the welding section), caramelize the sugar on top by moving the torch in swift, even motions over the top. If you're a klutz of are afraid of open flames, you can absolutely skip this step, but the caramelized sugar adds a nice crunch to the whole thing. Garnish with more fresh sliced figs and some fresh mint.

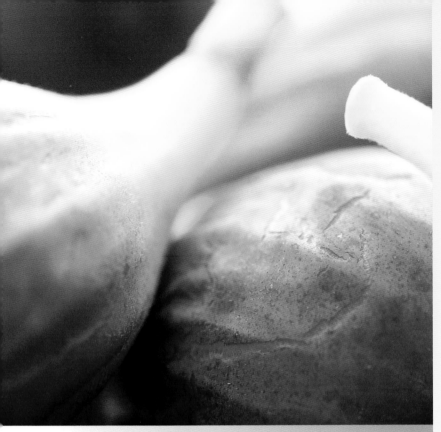

Figs in a Blanket Salad

Figs, ham, and cheese. It's hard to make those three ingredients taste bad in any combination, and they taste exceptionally well together in this arrangement. You can stuff the figs with any cheese you like, but I find that by combining the two distinct flavors of soft, fresh chevre and an upfront blue cheese, you end up with something new and altogether tasty. But please feel free to experiment with your favorite cheeses. And for the greens, something peppery like purslane or arugula pairs nicely with the sweet and salty tones of the figs and the dressing.

For the Figs:

5-6 large, firm, fresh figs
½ cup fresh chevre (I use the magnificent chevre from Sweet Grass Dairy)
½ cup blue cheese (I use Flat Creek's Farmhouse Blue)
5-6 slices of prosciutto, sliced paper thin
½ cup walnut halves
pepper, to taste

Let the cheeses sit out of the fridge until they're room temperature, then combine them with a crack or two of pepper in a food processor. If the cheeses are too thick, you can drizzle a little oil in to help them blend. Cut a deep X in the bottom if each fig and gently squeeze the opposite side so that the fig opens up a little. Place a walnut half in the middle then stuff the fig with the cheese mixture. Next, wrap each stuffed fig with a thin piece of prosciutto and secure it in place with a toothpick. You'll have to sneak the toothpick in alongside the walnut, but it'll work.

In a medium skillet over medium heat, gently sauté the stuffed figs until the prosciutto renders out a bit of its fat and the ham gets a little color on it. Remove the figs from the skillet and set them to the side while you work on the salad. Don't forget to remove the toothpicks!

For the dressing and salad:

3 tablespoons whole fig preserves
1 clove garlic
¼ cup red wine vinegar
½ cup avocado oil (or good quality olive oil)
Sea salt and pepper to taste
2-3 cups purslane or arugula
1 cup sunflower seed sprouts (or other tasty sprouts)

In a food processor, pulse together the fig preserves, garlic, vinegar, oil, and a pinch of salt and a grind or two of pepper. A few pulses are all it takes to blend the dressing into a smooth consistency. Different preserves have different viscosities (I've been waiting all day to say "viscosities"), so if it's too thick, thin the dressing down with a touch more vinegar or even a splash of water. Toss the dressing with the greens and sprouts at the last minute and serve with the warm fig bundles. Good stuff!

Grits

I love preparing grits for the uninitiated just to watch their facial expressions. Unless you were raised in the South, chances are you probably aren't a huge fan of this regional favorite. I've been a big fan of Logan Turnpike Grits for years and had a chance to incorporate them in the Figs episode of *Hans Cooks the South*. Not only was I able to witness the whole stone-ground mill process first hand, but owners George and Cecilia Holland gave me quite an education as well. I was always under the impression that the difference between polenta and grits was that polenta was ground corn and grits was ground hominy. Not true. Hominy is dried corn that's been soaked in either some sort of alkali (historically wood ash) to remove the germ and the hard outer husk, resulting in a more tender, easier to digest grain. I must admit, I've never been a big fan of hominy. Grits is simply ground, dried corn that's been milled to a coarse consistency. It's then cooked in either milk or water and becomes, essentially, corn porridge. It can be flavored with all sorts of good stuff like bacon, cheese, onions, salt, pepper, and even sugar.

On the show I made Vidalia Onion Grits and they really came out nicely. To make them, simply cook 1 large diced Vidalia onion with about ¼ cup of fig-infused, white balsamic vinegar. When the onions turn translucent and most of the vinegar had evaporated, simply stir those oniony-jewels into white or yellow stone-ground grits and you have the base for a fabulous meal. Try them with the Fig-Chipotle BBQ Quail, shrimp, or even a fried egg.

If you've not tried grits, start by trying really good, stone-ground grits and not that instant stuff. There really is no comparison. My friends Cecilia and George Holland would be happy to ship you some of their famous yellow or white speckled grits, no matter where you live. You can find Logan Turnpike online at: www.loganturnpikemill.com

Note: If something seems grammatically screwy with all of this grits talk, it's because the word grits is a singular noun. As awkward as it sounds, it's actually grammatically correct to say, "This Vidalia onion grits is good". I had to go back and correct myself like nine times and I probably still managed to flub it up somehow!

Half Full

I've always felt rather clever when I hear people discussing the old-as-dirt dilemma as to whether a glass is half-full or half-empty. Labeling myself a solid "realist" my answer has always been that a glass is half-full when you're in the process of filling it, and therefore half-empty when it's in the process of being emptied. So that glass of tea is half-empty if you're drinking it, and half-full when the waiter replenishes your tea to the 50 percent level (though his tip may suffer if he only half-fills your glass). Of course the half-full/half-empty debate is simply a metaphorical test meant to establish one's sense of optimism or pessimism. To be honest, there are days when it seems half-full, others when it seems half-empty, and possibly more still when you really just don't care. And then there are some days we don't even notice the glass or its contents.

But for those of us who've heard the words "you have cancer" the glass becomes suddenly lead-heavy and all too real. We realize that the glass is actually an hourglass and every grain of sand that falls lands like a boulder with a deafening thud. Of course no one is naïve enough to think they'll live forever. We all know that the sand is running in our hourglasses, our clocks are ticking. Life is a terminal condition they say, and it's true. But cancer, or any life-threatening illness, forces us to stare that hour glass down with an uncomfortable intensity that puts us face to face with our lives: our past, our present, and what may or may not be our future.

The term "half-full" holds an additional meaning for me. My cancer cost me half of my stomach and half of my esophagus, which means I'm half full after about three or four bites. But that same cancer that left my digestive bits in disarray also helped me to realize that it truly is our own perception that dictates the fullness of our glass. It's that epiphany, that paradigm shift that I think is so vital to those who've had the great misfortune to find themselves in the shadow of cancer.

You know, Hans has a subtle yet not so subtle way of reminding us all to take nothing for granted.

It was approximately three and a half years ago that our shared love for art caused our paths to cross.

Within a few months of that he would be diagnosed with stomach cancer.
A short while after that I would be asking him to ask his physician how he felt about sending Hans to M D Anderson Hospital in Houston for his surgery and treatments. And a few weeks after that I found myself entering the intensive care unit to say "Hello" to a man that had just experienced fourteen hours or so of major cancer surgery. I will never forget that image of Hans propped up in bed, tubes and all, welcoming me into his room. I knew at that very moment that Hans would be using his love of cooking and his outgoing personality to help others who would experience those same health issues that he had. That is exactly what he is doing. He has accomplished many things over the years however the love and help he offers to other cancer survivors is what I am most proud of. This cookbook is just another extension of those heartfelt efforts. Hans is a great friend to have. He has a minimum of a dozen projects all going at the same time and will be the first one to make you feel guilty if you might want to take a break from your own self perceived busy schedule. With Hans around you WILL get things done. Hans is practically a brother to Ron and me and it is with much pride that I write these words. I wonder if he will ever forgive me for serving him those pancakes from the box a few years back? Lots of love and admiration go out to Hans, Amy, Finn, and Ella.

-Don Bertram
"Celebrate Imagination"
Houston, Texas

I have a shirt that reads "Cancer Sucks!" and there's absolutely no denying that truth. Surgery, chemo, radiation, nausea, hair loss, energy loss and pain are not the kinds of tools you'd expect to find in an optimist's tool belt.

But once you emerge on the other side of that experience, the day-to-day "problems" that trouble people (traffic, weather, gossip, etc.) all seem somehow trivial. The truth of it is that if you even have the breath to debate the fullness of the glass, you have something (and surely several things) to be thankful for. It takes genuine effort to be an optimistic person and no effort at all to be a pessimist. I fall back into my old fault-finding ways from time to time and can always count on my wife to put things back in perspective for me. The silver lining is not always obvious, but I promise it's worth looking for.

Half-Kraut

With a name like Hans, you have to imagine that either there's a bit of German in my blood or, perhaps, that

my parents had a good sense of humor. As it turns out, both are true. My father Jochem (just call him Joe)

was born in 1940 in the northeast corner of Germany in a town that was later given to Poland after World

War II. After having escaped from East Germany in his twenties, he attended a hotel and catering school in

a picturesque Bavarian town near Munich called Tegensee. That experience eventually landed him a job in

Chicago at the Four Seasons restaurant at the O'Hare airport. He later found employment at the Francis

Marion Hotel in Charleston, South Carolina where he would eventually meet my mom, an Elvis-loving

Georgia Peach from Canon, Ga. (That story is worthy of its own book and maybe one day I'll

convince them to write it.)

So technically, I'm a Half-Kraut and German food and culture are essential ingredients in the recipe that yielded

who I am. In fact, I was a dual citizen of the U.S. and Germany until I was 18. When I was younger, we would

often travel to Germany for the holidays and I even spent a couple of summers there traveling around the

country with my cousins. Luckily, my overseas family enjoys a good meal and, knowing I was a restaurant boy,

they'd take me to experience fantastic examples of German cuisine (which includes, of course, beer!).

As in many countries, each region of Germany has its own specialty, so it's hard to define what exactly

Wiener Schnitzel

Some folks get confused when they hear Wiener Schnitzel. They think that a Wiener is a sausage, and it can be ... BUT, the word Wiener means "from Vienna", or Wien (pronounced 'veen'). So a Wienerwurst is a Viennese sausage and a Wiener Schnitzel is basically a breaded cutlet prepared the way they make it in Wien. I have a great Wiener Schnitzel story that involves an ignorant, angry customer, an even angrier chef, and the local police. But that's another story for another book ...

3 oz. trimmed veal (per person), pounded flat
Flour
Breadcrumbs
3 eggs beaten
Salt/Pepper

Simply season the pounded cutlets with salt and pepper, then dredge in flour, then into the beaten eggs, then into the breadcrumbs, making sure that the cutlets are complete dry. Sautee the cutlets in clarified butter until golden brown and crunchy. Blot on paper towels.

Traditionally, Wiener Schnitzel is garnished with a lemon slice topped with a mixture of diced onions, tomatoes, scallions, and some capers. Then lay an anchovy fillet over the top of that and you're good to go. Alternatively, you can add two sunny-side up fried eggs on top and you'll have Wiener Schnitzel ala Holstein ... mmm!

Spaetzle

The word spaetzle means "little sparrows" and they're essentially German drop noodles or dumplings and they're brilliant. Extremely versatile, you can create variations by adding things to the basic dough. Try adding some mashed sweet potatoes, spinach, or even your favorite cheese for a nice twist.

What you need:
2 cups all-purpose flour
2 whole eggs-beaten
⅔ cup water
½ teaspoon white pepper-ground
pinch nutmeg-ground
½ teaspoon salt

In a large bowl, combine flour, white pepper, nutmeg, and salt. Form a well in the center of the flour mixture and add eggs. Slowly combine eggs and flour by bringing in the sides of the well. Add water as the dough thickens. You may use more or less water depending on your type of flour, but the resulting dough should have the consistency of really thick paste. Spoon the dough onto a wet cutting board and with a long knife, "cut" the dough into the boiling water in strips and let boil for 3-4 minutes. After cooking, strain spaetzle into an ice bath to halt the cooking process. Drain spaetzle thoroughly. For service, simply sauté in a little butter until the edges just start to brown.

.

German food is. It has a reputation for being heavy, and in truth, it can be. Slow-cooked meats, sausages, root vegetables, and cabbage are common, but that's not the extent of the cuisine. Wild mushrooms, berries, spring greens, and fresh fish are common on the spiesekarte, though we rarely hear about those specialties here in the States. One thing you'll find common throughout Germany is their love of sweet, sour, and salty. Vinegar, sugar, and salt find their way into not only the main courses, but sides like Bavarian Red Cabbage or even a vinaigrette for a salad.

Soon after my cancer diagnosis, I realized that I wanted to connect my children with their family overseas. My cousin and dear friend Tobi organized a family reunion and we all met the week before Easter in the beautiful city of Celle. Despite somewhat of a language barrier, all of the children instantly bonded, playing together as if they'd known each other for years. The kids connected with the country as well, absorbing the castles, museums and the cuisine into their own personal sense of culture. We're already planning our return visit and the children simply cannot wait. I hope their heritage is as important to them as it has been to me.

Here are just a few of my favorite German dishes made ,perhaps, with a lighter hand. My father jokes that most Americans think that Germans only eat in October, but there's nothing wrong with a good German meal anytime of the year.

Bavarian Red Cabbage

There's nothing worse than going to a German restaurant and being served canned red cabbage. It's an insult, especially when you've tasted the real thing. Sweet, spicy, and rich with the promise of good things to come, there's nothing like the smell of red cabbage simmering for hours on the cook top.

6 slices bacon, diced
2 large yellow onions, sliced
2 Red cabbage, 2 heads sliced
¼ cup Worcestershire sauce
½ cup cider or tarragon vinegar
¾ cup sugar
¼ cup salt
¼ cup coarse ground peppercorn
teaspoon each: ground cloves, allspice, cinnamon
4 bay leaves
Salt/Pepper

In a large pot, add the ingredients in this order: bacon, onions, cabbage, spices, bay leaves, sugar, salt, and pepper. Then add your vinegar and Worcestershire sauce to wash those spices down into the pot. Place the pot on medium heat for about 5 minutes, then reduce to a simmer and cook for about 2 hours, stirring once or twice AFTER the first hour.

Fritatten Suppe

How can you go wrong with a soup that's full of crepes? I always look forward to the roadside restaurants as we travel across Germany, each one with their own take on this traditional soup. Savory pancakes sliced thin in a warm broth. I think I'll make some now…

For the crepes:

3 eggs (beaten)
1 teaspoon or so of flour

For the soup:

6-8 cups chicken stock
Assorted soup veggies (if desired): carrots, celery, parsnips, onions, etc.
2 cups romaine lettuce, chopped
1 cup sliced mushrooms (if desired)

Add a splash of water to the beaten eggs and then add the flour and combine. You're essentially making REALLY thin pancake batter. At this point, you can add all sorts of things from fresh herbs to cracked pepper, but for your first batch, start simple. Make as many thin crepes as you can. When the crepes cool, slice them into long, thin strips and set those to the side. The soup stock can be flavored with anything you like, but typically it's just a lightly salted, clear chicken stock.
In a sauté pan, heat a little of olive oil until almost smoking. Add your romaine lettuce and toss until barely wilted. If you're adding mushrooms, do a quick sauté of those as well.

To serve, pile in your sliced crepes, then top with the seared romaine and mushrooms and finally, ladle the stock to fill the bowl. Serve immediately. You can keep leftover crepes in the freezer and add them to future bowls of Frittaten suppe.

Kaiserschmarrn

Anyone who likes sweets owes it to themself to travel to Salzburg, Austria. People say they go for Mozart and the castles and the churches, but they're really just there for the heavy curtained coffee houses with their unbelievable desserts. Salzburg's best known desserts are the sinfully chocolate Dobostorte and the mountainous lemon soufflé known as Salzburger Knockerln. On one of my visits, however, I fell in love with Kaiserschmarrn, a simple dish that looks like what might happen if you flung a pancake into a ceiling fan. Here's a simple recipe that requires no ceiling fan.

4 eggs, separated
1 cups flour
1 cups milk
pinch of salt
2 tablespoons sugar
½ cup golden raisins
3 tablespoons rum
confectioner's sugar
Almonds

First, soak your raisins in the rum. Then whisk together the egg yolks and the sugar. Slowly whisk in the milk and then the flour, whisking out any lumps but not over beating. Let this mix sit while you beat the egg whites to stiff peaks in a separate bowl. Slowly fold the beaten whites into the other mixture and add a pinch of salt and sugar. Melt a generous amount of butter in your favorite pancake pan and proceed as if you're making pancakes (because you are). When the butter's hot, pour or ladle enough batter to cover the bottom of the pan. As the bottom begins to brown, sprinkle your rum-soaked raisins all over the pancake. Flip the pancake when the bottom is nice and golden. Right when the pancake finishes, turn off the heat and tear it into strips in the pan with two forks. It's supposed to be all torn and choppy so don't try to make things even. Transfer the mutilated pancake to a plate and top it with sliced almonds and confectioner's sugar. When you're finished, call me and I'll be right over. This recipe makes enough for three large pancakes, so don't be greedy.

Gesundheit!

Isn't that just something you say when people sneeze? Doesn't that mean God bless you? Gesundheit is simply

a wish for good health, almost like a toast to your health. So when someone sneezes, you're wishing that they

get healthy. After all of the health issues I've been through, I figure the best thing I can do for anyone is to wish

them good health. It's something we all take for granted, but without your health, what do you have? And the

inspiring thing is that what we eat can help determine how healthy we are. The human immune system is an

amazing thing, but it needs all the help it can get from the vitamins, nutrients, and enzymes found in foods. So

when I say "gesundheit" I'm not just wishing good health for you, but urging you to take charge of your health.

Don't wait for a bout with bad health to start taking preventative measures toward improving your quality of life.

I'm no doctor, but I'd like to offer you this simple prescription: Eat Well, Feel Well and Thrive.

you NEED to Be where you Can be the person you NEED to BE

Un-boring Salads

At some point during the strange and wonderful evolution of American cuisine, salads took a sad turn for the worse. Earthy greens were replaced by bland and virtually nutrition-less Iceberg salads, garnished with the obligatory tomato, shredded carrots and, if you're lucky, a slice of cucumber. Light and silky vinaigrettes were replaced by obscene globs of egg-heavy, or sometimes even gelatinous dressings. Now don't get me wrong... I love Thousand Island and Ranch as much as the next person, and the crunch of Iceberg lettuce cannot be rivaled. But these often-uninspired arrangements have somehow come to define the American salad and that's an unfortunate trend that I'd like to help thwart.

Salads are easy... Mother Nature has already packed her greens with tremendous flavors, but sometimes they simply need a little coaxing to bring out their full potential. Local grocers are now carrying some really nice organic greens, including a nice Spring Mix that usually includes baby spinach, frisée, beet greens, baby arugula (my favorite), and red leaf lettuce among others. Despite the seasonality of its name, Spring Mix is greenhouse grown and is available all year round. You'll be amazed at the variety of greens available at your local farmers' market.

Ultimately, a salad dressing should enhance the inherent and unique flavors of the greens, not mask them. If you're tossing the salad, you want the dressing to just coat the leaves, not drown them. Most egg or mayonnaise-based dressing should really be served on the side so that each person can administer it to their personal tastes. Whatever your preference, remember to add some personality to your salads... after all, you are what you eat.

Coffee Molasses Vinaigrette

This dressing was inspired by an excess of espresso that was just too good to toss out.

1 tablespoon molasses
¼ cup white balsamic vinegar
½ cup avocado oil or olive oil
1-2 cloves of garlic
1 shot of Espresso
Salt/Pepper

Whisk together above ingredients and toss with your favorite greens. The slight bittersweet flavors in this dressing work well with slightly bitter greens like endive, escarole, or radicchio.

Garlic Pomegranate Vinaigrette

For the dressing:
2 teaspoons minced garlic
1 tablespoon pomegranate molasses (or standard molasses)
¼ teaspoon sea salt
¼ teaspoon fresh cracked pepper
¼ cup pomegranate juice
¼ cup white balsamic vinegar (or white wine vinegar)
½ cup olive oil

In a Mason jar or cruet, simple shake all the ingredients vigorously until well combined. Drizzle or toss dressing with your favorite greens and serve with grilled chicken, fish, or even heart healthy red beans.

Our Little Garden

The best way to connect yourself to the food you eat is to grow some for yourself. There are a million reasons to convince yourself why you shouldn't have a garden (I don't have time, my yard is too small, I don't have a yard, etc.), but all it takes is one bite of a homegrown tomato and you'll find a way to grow some food. If you are one of those yard-less people, there are all sorts of modern, indoor growing contraptions that will allow you to grow simple crops like herbs or even small tomatoes. You may be surprised to know how efficient container gardening can be, allowing you to produce an inspiring amount of food on your back porch or patio. Better yet, there's probably a community garden in your area where you can, often for a small donation, "own" a small plot of land where you can get your hands dirty and enjoy the full benefits of gardening. My friend John Silk introduced me to the wonderful folks at the Oakhurst community garden near the Atlanta suburb of Decatur. Each plot overflows with an amazing array of herbs and vegetables, from the everyday to the exotic. Not only does it give you a source of fresh food, it roots you to your community in ways you never would've imagined. And, like Oakhurst, many community gardens in large metropolitan areas make it a point to share the joy of gardening with children who would otherwise not have the opportunity to witness the magic of tiny seeds bursting to life and producing beautiful and delicious foods.

Gingered Sugar Snaps
with Shallots

Simple, fresh, delicious, but the best part is, the kids
actually request them on a regular basis. No frowny
faces here ... just big, sugar-snappy smiles.

2 tablespoons butter
1 tablespoon avocado oil
2 cups sugar snaps (strings removed)
3 shallots, sliced
1 tablespoon garlic
1 tablespoon ginger
Salt to taste

Heat butter and oil over medium-high heat, add
ginger and garlic and sauté for about 30 seconds. Add
shallots and cook until translucent. Add sugar snaps
and flash heat until just hot but still crunchy. Season
with salt and enjoy!

Seared Romaine & Cucumber

This is another one inspired by my father's supernatural ability to take what's on hand and create something unforgettable. You'll be pleasantly impressed at how a little heat can transform a couple of old salad ingredients into something so vibrant.

Butter
1 head Romaine lettuce, chopped
2 Cucumbers, peeled, seeded, and cubed
¼ teaspoon ground turmeric
½ cup diced Yellow Onion
1 teaspoon grated Ginger
juice and zest of one lemon
Salt

In a heavy skillet or wok over high flame, heat about 2 tablespoon butter until nearly smoking. Add grated ginger and onion and cook for 1 minute over high heat. Add chopped Romaine and stir until just seared and wilted. Toss in turmeric and cucumber. Remove from heat when cucumber is just warmed through. Add the lemon juice and zest, season with a good pinch of sea salt and enjoy.

I kept a rather large and unruly garden at our previous house in the tiny village of Tate, Ga. There, a century of oak leaves naturally mulched to form a loose, coffee-colored soil where our raspberries flourished and arugula and lemon balm sprouted between the pavers in the walkway. I called it the "Garden of Reckless Abandon," not because it was neglected in anyway, but because the fecundity of the soil made it impossible to maintain. You could almost watch the seedlings reach for the sky, unfurling pale green leaves to drink in the sun's steady supply of warmth and energy, while beneath, pale roots scrambled down into the mineral-rich darkness. I firmly believe that weeds would vacation in that garden, enjoying that dark soil as much as pale tourists enjoy a sandy beach.

We outgrew our little bungalow and traded in that house for life in a relatively new neighborhood. We only have room for a tiny garden and when our shovel first met Earth in our new backyard, it struck a powerful combination of red-clay and stubborn rocks, Bermuda grass runners and ill-tempered dandelions. We've worked hard to amend the soil, adding rich composted manure, topsoil, and mulch so that we can continue to enjoy the rewards of gardening. Our modest garden is only about a fifth the size of our last plot, but we still manage to produce a considerable amount of food in that compact area. The goal of our little garden isn't quantity. In other words, we're not trying to grow enough food to last through the winter or to feed an army. Instead, our goal is quality. We rifle through seed catalogs each year searching for new varieties or heirloom favorites, counting the days until the soil is warm enough to accept them. The children watch the garden each day, fueling the seedlings' growth with their wide-eyed enthusiasm and love. Once talk of Star Wars and Hello Kitty die down, Finn and Ella always take visiting children to the garden to let their friends experience the licorice kiss of freshly pinched fennel fronds or the unrivaled crunch of a sweet pepper picked right from the plant. No matter how large or how productive it may happen to be, each garden is unique, each home to a certain magic that reconnects us to our roots.

Japanese Eggplant Baba Ghanoush

I love to grow Japanese eggplants in the garden. They're long, slender, uniform in shape and an absolutely beautiful shade of purple. I love them simply grilled with a little oil and sea salt. I typically save up a few and grill them all at one time to make baba ghanoush. It's easy and delicious, and it's just fun to say "baba ghanoush" again and again in my Yogi Bear voice. Simple pleasures…

There's nothing to mess up here. Just slice the eggplants thinly lengthwise and drizzle them with some good quality oil. Sprinkle them with some coarse sea salt and cook them in a grill pan or on the upper rack of your grill. The skin can burn somewhat easily, so turn them as soon as they start to caramelize. When they're cooked through and somewhat soft, pulverize them in a food processor with as much garlic as you can stand. I usually roast an entire head of garlic while I'm cooking the eggplant and put the whole thing in there (minus the papery outside of course). If you're using raw garlic, you'll probably want to use 3-5 cloves. As the food processor is spinning, drizzle enough oil in the machine to make a nice, smooth paste. Season with more sea salt and cracked pepper and dig in. Baba ghanoush is great on toast, crackers, as a dip for vegetables, or even on a grilled piece of fish. I can't wait for my next batch of eggplants.

Black-Eyed Pea Salad

It's amazing how many peas a few vines can produce. We pushed about eight beans in the ground and harvested black-eyed peas all summer long. If you don't have fresh peas on hand, simply soak dried beans overnight to rehydrate them. I made this salad for a party once and watched as most people avoided it like the plague, filling their plates instead with cheese curls and Doritos. The folks that did try the salad loved it, and I think you will too. It's one of those things that really tastes better the day after you make it, the flavors opening up and really getting to know each other as they spend time together in the bowl.

1 pound black-eyed peas, fresh or rehydrated
1 fennel bulb, diced (fronds reserved)
4 roma tomatoes, diced
1 cup Vidalia onion, diced
1 tablespoon Out of the Blue salt
1 teaspoon ground cumin
2 teaspoons ground coriander
¼ cup olive oil
3 tablespoons white balsamic vinegar

In a large pot, cover the peas with cold water and bring to a rolling boil. Reduce the heat to a low boil and cook for 10-15 minutes or until the peas are just tender, but still hold their shape. You don't want mushy peas! Drain the peas and give them a quick rinse with cold water. Put the peas in the fridge and let them get nice and cold. When chilled, combine the peas with the rest of the ingredients. Finely chop the reserved fennel fronds and add them to the salad as well. I've found that some peas, for whatever reason, just need a little more salt than others, so be sure to adjust the seasoning to your liking. Cover and refrigerate for at least 1 hour, making sure to give the whole thing a thorough mix-up before service.

Garden Friends

Our decision to refrain from using pesticides in our garden was one that was fueled, primarily, by health concerns. With my cancer history, I don't want to fool around with potentially toxic substances meant to destroy a living creature, even if I don't share the same number of legs as the intended target of those poisons. The result of that decision is, guess what, we have bugs! And not just bugs, but the creatures that eat bugs (which, as it turns out, are often also bugs). Our little garden is home to all sorts of critters, from grasshoppers to mantis, from fat toads to dragonflies, every inch of green space is alive with creatures interested in sharing in our backyard bounty. Our strategy for dealing with these critters? Well, I guess we just let them be. If I have a blemish on my tomato where a shield bug took a small bite, then I'll just cut off that spot when I'm slicing the tomato for my sandwich. If I see a few aphids on my black-eyed pea pods, then I know I can expect a fat and sassy ladybug to come by soon for some natural "pest" control. When the ants demolish one of my prize figs … well … OK … that does upset me a bit, but in truth, there will be enough for everyone in the end. Healthy plants have their own means of self-defense, so the best strategy is to keep those plants healthy and let Mother Nature take care of the rest.

And when you really stop and look at them, our garden friends are truly beautiful. Rather than stalking the celery with Sevin dust, I arm myself with my camera and a macro lens and hunt for the hidden universe between the fronds of green. It's amazing what you'll find out there if you just look.

Reservoir Frogs

Our back deck sports a motley collection of self-watering planters where we grow parsley, nasturtiums, little roma tomatoes, or whatever strikes our fancy. These containers look like regular terracotta planters, but they have a reservoir bottom that allows the plants roots to access water as they need it. For the last several years, our largest reservoir planter has been home to one laid-back little tree frog. When the temperature is scalding hot outside, our froggy friend lounges in the water like he's waiting for me to bring him a fruity beverage … you know, something with an umbrella in it. We have several tree frogs in the tree that shades our deck, and I wonder if they have little pool parties when we're not looking. I can't see down into the reservoir, but I have to think that our self-watering planter is home to countless pollywogs, a sacred place where the next generation can emerge and take to the trees to sing their simple songs. If we used chemical fertilizers or pesticides on crops, our little tree-hugging, liquid-loving friends would take their party elsewhere. It goes without saying, our back deck would never be the same. Long live the reservoir frogs!

Blooming!

Flowers make people happy. I know that seems overly simple, but surrounding ourselves with flowers is an easy way to inject a little sunshine into our lives. I grew up in the shadow of my flower-obsessed father who was forever bringing in bromeliads or orchids from the greenhouse for us to enjoy their ephemeral blooms, returning them to greenhouse once again when their blooms were spent. My wife Amy always makes sure we have something blooming in the house, either living or arranged. It's just a little detail that makes our home feel … well, homey. I'm always on the lookout for discounted orchids or bromeliads, usually finding them for just a few bucks once their blooms are spent. These rescued plants add nice splashes of green throughout the house, but the nice thing is that they'll eventually re-bloom or, in the case of bromeliads, make new plants that will come up and bloom in turn. The promise of lush blooms is something to look forward to again and again, and it just makes you feel good.

Honey

I've read that bees travel over 55,000 miles and visit over 2 million blossoms to gather enough nectar to produce just one pound of honey. Yet we swat at them when they come buzzing around our picnic table! I suggest the next time you see a bee, you stop and thank it for all its hard work! I love seeing them rustling through our little garden, their fuzzy legs heavy with pollen. I hope they enjoy my flowers as much as I enjoy their honey.

Locally-produced honey is said to help alleviate certain allergies, but even if that were just a rumor, I'd still eat the stuff on everything. Honey is a known antiseptic and has been used for centuries to help heal wounds and suppress coughs. Of course honey makes the perfect sweetener for baking, but try incorporating it into your favorite savory dishes as well. Support your local beekeepers, buy some local honey, and enjoy the hard work of all those busy little bees.

Honey Feta Vinaigrette

This is a beautiful, silky dressing that plays on both the sweetness of the honey and the salty twang of good feta. Depending on the variety of feta used, you may want to add just a pinch of salt to the finished dressing.

2 tablespoon local honey
¼ cup white balsamic vinegar
½ cup avocado oil or olive oil
2 cloves of garlic
½ cup feta cheese (preferably goat or sheep's milk)

Combine ingredients in a blender or food processor and serve over your favorite greens with some extra feta for good measure. It's also exceptionally good in pasta salads as well.

Chocolate Honey Crème Brulee

This is a stripped down version of the classic crème brulee, but one I think you'll make a bit more often. And when chocolate and honey get together, you know you're going to end up with something good.

12 oz. evaporated milk
1 cup whole milk
2 eggs
½ cup honey
1 tablespoon cocoa powder or grated chocolate
2 teaspoons grated orange peel
1 teaspoon vanilla
1 tablespoon raw sugar (for caramel top)

In a large bowl, beat eggs, whole milk, and evaporated milk together until well blended. Add honey, cocoa powder, orange peel, and vanilla. Divide mixture evenly into ovenproof ramekins or custard cups and place in a baking pan. Pour boiling water into baking pan until it reaches half way up the ramekins. Bake at 325°F for 1 hour or until knife inserted in center comes out clean. Carefully remove from water bath and refrigerate for 4 hours or overnight. To serve, sprinkle an even layer of sugar on the tops of the brulees and caramelize with either a torch or directly under a broiler.

Okra

Okra is a great divider. Say the word in a crowded room and you'll quickly split the group into two factions: those who grin and salivate and those who contort their faces and wince. I've been an okra lover since my first taste of cornmeal crusted fried okra as a little boy sitting at my grandmother's kitchen table. I'd watch her shake the green pods in a paper bag with a little cornmeal, then fry them off in an electric skillet. Her entire house smelled like heaven as I ate the crunchy bites with my fingers, plucking them straight off of a paper towel-lined plate. In the hot months she planted okra seeds in her front flower bed. I'd watch them all summer long, anxiously waiting for their butter yellow flowers to give way to green, finger-like pods. It's been a life-long love affair and I'll eat okra boiled, stewed, pickled, fried, and even raw in a salad. If it's true that you are what you eat, then I am okra.

But for some people (those contorted-face folks I mentioned earlier), okra means one thing: SLIME. When it's heated, okra produces a sticky, stringy substance called mucilage. That's not a pretty word, is it? Mucilage from okra is used in industrial and medical applications and has even been used as a plasma replacement and blood volume expander. But let's talk about the culinary side of the plant, shall we? Okra's sticky properties make it a useful tool in the kitchen when thickening soups, stews, and gumbos. In fact, the word gumbo is derived from the West African word for okra. But if it's cooked fast and furiously, that slime you're worried about (which folks around here sometimes call "roping") is virtually non-existent and the pods burst in your teeth like no other vegetable.

Honey-Cumin Okra

My favorite way to eat okra is to simply flash heat it with a few spices until the pods are hot but still crunchy. If you have an aversion to okra, give this recipe a try. I've converted quite a few folks over to okra with this one.

2 cups okra pods, capped and halved
1 fat clove of garlic, rough chopped
¼ teaspoon ground cumin
¼ teaspoon sea salt
¼ teaspoon coarse ground pepper
2 tablespoon honey
2 tablespoon olive oil

Heat the olive oil on high heat and fry the garlic until it just starts to brown. Add okra, cumin, salt, and pepper and toss until just heated through. Turn off heat and add honey, tossing to cover. Serve immediately. When you cook it this fast, it doesn't have a chance to get slimy and it has a great crunch. For a twist, add a solid dash of your favorite hot sauce. The combination of sweet, hot, and crunch is downright addictive. Give it a try...

Green Gumbo

Monkfish is sometimes called 'poor man's lobster' because the meat has a firm consistency like that of a lobster's tail. If you can't find it, substitute with farm-raised catfish cut into cubes. And what is Solomon Gundy? Well, you have to experience this Caribbean smoked herring paste to fully appreciate it. It's entirely optional, but it adds a deep smokiness to the dish that's hard to match. I did a dish very similar to this one on my application video for the Next Food Network Star and have had tons of people tell me how much they love Solomon Gundy now.

1 tablespoon butter
1 tablespoon oil
1 medium onion, diced large
1 teaspoon garlic, minced
½ cup flour
1- 8oz. fillet of monkfish, cut into ½ inch cubes
2 cups sliced fresh okra
1 large green-when-ripe tomato, diced
1 teaspoon Solomon Gundy (optional)
1 cucumber, peeled, halved, and chunked
1 cup shrimp, peeled and deveined
½ cup stock (I make a simple shrimp stock using the shrimp shells,
but chicken or vegetable stock will work fine)
salt/pepper

In a large skillet, heat the butter and oil over medium-high until it's nearly smoking. Add onions and 1 tsp of Solomon Gundy (if using). Cook until onions, stirring constantly, until the onion begins to brown on the edges. Dust the monkfish pieces in flour and sauté them in the skillet. As soon as they start to brown, flip the fish and add the shrimp, tomato, and cucumber. As soon as the shrimp turn just a little pink, add the okra. Be sure to keep the pan moving by either flipping the ingredients or keeping them in motion with a wooden spoon. As soon as the okra is heated through, add the stock and adjust your seasoning with salt and pepper. If you're using Solomon Gundy, you probably won't need much more salt, but check it anyway. Serve the gumbo in a shallow bowl over couscous, grits or rice.

Spinach

Did you ever stop and wonder why Popeye just didn't eat the spinach at the beginning of the cartoon instead of waiting 'til he was nearly down for the count? After all those years of being clobbered by a spinach-fueled Popeye, don't you think Bluto would've tried a can of the stuff himself? I guess cartoons don't have to make much sense, but if there's a moral to be harvested from those old Popeye cartoons, it's EAT YOUR SPINACH.

Spinach is arguably one of the most nutritious foods on the planet, packed with calcium, folic acid, vitamins A, C, and E, and even a bit of iron. Like many leafy greens, many of the plants nutritional values are compromised when you over cook it, so Popeye might have been better off with a handful of fresh leaves, or even a box of the frozen stuff. In any case, he was on to something.

But despite the cartoon's attempts to glorify spinach, most folks just don't like it. My guess is that they were served that grey-brown, canned, mushy stuff when they were kids and decided early on that spinach (at least in that form) is evil. So let me see if I can't change a few minds here with recipe using fresh spinach. When buying fresh spinach, look for bunches that have sturdy, clean leaves that are free from any dark or wilted patches. Fresh spinach smells wonderfully green, so employ your nose when choosing the best bunch. Bunch spinach should be stemmed and washed before use to remove any dirt that may have hitchhiked from the farm. Most markets now carry spinach that's already clipped and washed, but make sure to examine each bag to make sure that the leaves look crisp and healthy. Just a couple of black or mushy leaves in the bag can ruin the flavor of the entire lot, so steer clear of any bags containing questionable leaves.

Creamed Spinach

Spinach is amazing simply steamed with a little lemon juice, but if you're craving something a bit more substantial, it's hard to beat this steakhouse classic.

1 fat clove garlic, sliced
3 slices bacon, diced
¼ tsp grated nutmeg
10 oz. pkg. baby spinach leaves
¼ cup organic sour cream
2 tablespoons grated parmesan cheese

In a large skillet on medium heat, sweat the garlic and the bacon until the bacon turns translucent and the fat renders out. Grate the nutmeg into the pan, add the spinach, stir and cover. Cook for 2-3 minutes until the leaves begin to wilt. Add the sour cream and cheese and stir combine. Top with a bit more fresh grated Parmesan cheese and enjoy!

Cows Eat Grass…

Will Harris. No matter where I traveled in the state of Georgia, anytime local, organic, and sustainable foods were being discussed, the name Will Harris always came up. Several people even referred to Will Harris as the "rock star" of local food. When I finally had the opportunity to make my way down to Bluffton, Ga. to visit with Will at his fifth-generation farm, the "rock star" moniker seemed to catch the good-natured cowboy off guard. He instantly chuckled and shrugged off the accolade, but I could tell it made him swell with a bit of well-deserved pride. Will's family has been caring for cattle on their family farm since the time of reconstruction and his pride runs deeper than the roots of the white oaks that shade his pastures.

The grass-fed beef movement is gaining momentum across the country as wise consumers (like us) demand more from our food suppliers. Grass-fed beef may not be as tender as grain-fed, but it more than makes up for that in flavor. In addition, because a cow's digestion system is not equipped to process grain, there are some health issues associated with feeding them something other than their natural diet of grass. As well as causing increased flatulence, the all-grain diet establishes the perfect growing condition for the infamous and tenacious E. coli bacteria, which can often finds its way into the production process, contaminating the meat.

If you find yourself craving a little beef, take the extra effort to look for your local grass-fed beef supplier. You can find it in more and more markets these days and if you don't find it, ask for it.

Pan-seared Top Sirloin with Mustard-Red Wine pan sauce

You know that dark, often sticky stuff that's left at the bottom of the pan when you sear steaks? Well, believe it or not, that stuff (called fond) is delicious and is the base for many a delicious and genuinely effortless pan sauce. So grab your trusty wooden spoon and let's make something tasty!

2 10 oz. grass-fed, top sirloin steaks
½ cup Vidalia onions, diced
2 shallots, diced
½ teaspoon salt
¾ cup red wine
1 tablespoon mustard
1 tablespoon Worcestershire sauce
2 tablespoons butter
1-2 teaspoons fresh cracked pepper
oil

Marinate the steaks in a little oil and about ½ tablespoon of Worcestershire sauce. You can do this several hours in advance in the refrigerator, but ideally your steaks should be at or near room temperature when you're ready to cook. Heat a heavy skillet on high heat and give the steaks a good sear, turning only once the steaks are nice and brown on the first side. Cook for about 2-3 minutes on each side. Grass-fed beef is best served at medium or below. Turn the heat on the skillet down to a simmer and remove the steaks to a plate. Letting the steaks rest for a few moments really makes a difference in how tender they are. Add the onions and shallots to the pan and sauté for just a moment, really scraping and pushing the bottom of the skillet with a wooden spoon to loosen the fond. Add the wine, mustard, remaining Worcestershire sauce, salt and pepper. Turn up the heat to about medium-high and reduce the volume of the liquid by about half. Add any juices from the steak that have collected on the plate, then turn off the heat. Add the butter and stir until the butter is fully incorporated. The addition of the butter at the last minute will give the sauce a velvety texture and shine. Adjust the sauce for seasoning and simply serve over the steaks. Any remaining sauce would taste excellent on some mashed or roasted potatoes.

Georgia on a Vine - Persimmon Creek

A grape is a bit like a time capsule, each berry faithfully recording the story of the season in which it was reared. From the sun, wind, and rain down to the microbes in the soil, every nuance of the grapes' growing conditions affect the flavor and complexity of the fruit. When the grapes are processed into wine, those subtleties are transferred into glass bottles where they will once again be subject to light, temperature, and time. When you really think about the amount of effort that goes into each bottle, wine starts to look less like fermented grape juice and more like a feat of pure alchemy.

Having never visited a vineyard, and especially not a Georgia vineyard, I really had no expectations. I am by no means a wine snob, but I can appreciate quality. Owner Mary Ann Hardman is quick to point out that wine doesn't grow on the vine, and behind every bottle is a vineyard. She'll also be the first to tell you that dirt is sexy! At Persimmon Creek, each bottle is the result of dedication, hard work, patience, a unique microclimate, and a whole bunch of love. The Hardmans have created something larger than the wine and I'd encourage you to make the journey to Clayton, Ga. if you get the chance. Persimmon Creek and its North Georgia peers are working hard to create great wines that the whole world can enjoy.

Of course the next harvest at Persimmon Creek will be a few grapes shy after I made the rounds at the vineyard. The grapes are so abundant and so delicious that I was starting to wonder if the bird netting was there to protect the vines from marauding birds or hungry visitors like myself. Each variety has such unique characteristics, so sweet, sour, and burstingly juicy, that it's hard not to sample them all and imagine how those qualities will manifest in each of their respective bottles. It's a long, labor-intensive process, but I think it's worth the wait.

Ricotta Custard with Spiced Red Wine Poached Pears

This fantastically easy custard has all the qualities of cheesecake without all of the fuss. Make sure to save the poaching liquid … it's delicious served warm with the custards.

For the Pears:

2 large, ripe pears, peeled, halved and cored
2 cups good red wine
3 cinnamon sticks
Peel from 1 orange
1 teaspoon whole cloves
2 teaspoons raw sugar

For the Custard:

8 ounces cream cheese , softened
⅓ cup fresh ricotta cheese
1 large egg , plus 1 large egg white
¼ cup sugar
¼ cup ½ & ½
¼ teaspoon vanilla extract

To make custard:

Preheat oven to 250°. In a heavy-duty mixing bowl, beat cream cheese until smooth and fluffy. Add the ricotta, then gradually beat in egg and egg white until smooth. Add the sugar, heavy cream and vanilla and beat until well blended.

Divide the mixture evenly into six 4-ounce ramekins or custard cups. Place ramekins in a large roasting pan and pour enough very hot water to come halfway up sides of ramekins. Bake for about 45 minutes or until the custards are just set. Transfer ramekins to wire rack to cool. Cover and refrigerate for about 3 hours, or overnight.

For the poached pears:
In a heavy saucepan, add all the ingredients and bring the heat up until the wine is just below the boil. Turn the heat down and simmer the pears until they're just knife tender. The longer the pears stay in the poaching liquid, the more flavor they will absorb.

To serve, simply slice the pears and serve on top of the custard. Delicious!

Recycling Foods – a.k.a. Lovely Leftovers

A good meal is only really good once. You can package away its remains in hopes of resurrecting it in the future, but ultimately it will only be a shadow of the meal it once was: the meat now dry and leathery, the once fluffy mashed potatoes now dense as clay, and the vegetables gone limp and lifeless. Many fine meals have waited in their cold plastic coffins until their creators gather enough resolve to finally throw them away.

The ability to utilize leftovers, to reincarnate them into something new and delicious, is one mark of a good cook. Rather than attempting to reheat the meal as a whole, try looking at each of its components as a new ingredient. Tear apart the remains of your once juicy roast chicken, saving the meat for quesadillas and the bones for stock. Last Tuesday's carrots transform easily into tonight's Gingered Carrot Bisque. Also, uneaten or abandoned shrimp lend themselves effortlessly to a nice shrimp salad or thrown in with some Seared Romaine and Cucumber to create an impromptu meal. While I'm ecstatic when my family or friends return to the kitchen for seconds or thirds, a part of me hopes there will be some leftovers that I can play with the next day.

Indian Spiced
Potato-Carrot Flitters

Root vegetables (like carrots, potatoes, parsnips, celeriac, and others) often contain high amounts of natural sugars and work well with spices such as cinnamon, cardamom, turmeric, cloves, and star anise. You can find a ready-made spice blend called Garam Masala in most markets that's truly worth picking up for your spice cabinet. If you can't find it, use a mild curry powder and omit the turmeric in the following preparation. Serve these mildly sweet flitters with some good applesauce or homemade apple butter.

2 large carrots (approx.), cooked until soft
3 large baking potatoes, cooked, peeled, and roughly mashed
2 tablespoon sour cream
½ teaspoon Garam Masala
1 teaspoon ground turmeric
2 large eggs
½ teaspoon baking powder
¼ cup whole milk
1 teaspoon cinnamon sugar
4 tablespoon all-purpose flour (approx.)
unsalted butter

In a large bowl or mixer, combine the first nine ingredients until well incorporated. It's ok to have some small chunks of carrot or potato in the mix. Add flour one tablespoon at a time while stirring. Depending on the starchiness of the potato, you may need more or less flour. Heat about 2 tablespoons of butter in a sauté pan (preferably non-stick) and cook the batter just as you would pancakes.

It was in that playful spirit that flitters were born. I'd always heard the expression "flat as a flitter", but had no idea what a flitter was. Rather than take the time or exert the effort to actually find out the true meaning of the term, I applied the name to a flat fritter (somewhat of a mutant pancake really) that I'd created using leftovers. The best thing about flitters is that they are tremendously versatile. Corn, rice, beans, carrots, chickpeas, spinach, potatoes of any variety, Lima beans, cooked salmon, crawfish tails, tomatoes, onions … the list of suitable candidates for a good flitter is almost endless.

The basic flitter recipe (if you can even call it a recipe) is perfectly simple and endlessly adaptable. In fact, it has to be since you never know what quantity you'll be left with. Essentially all we're doing is binding the chosen ingredients together with a couple of eggs, a bit of flour, and a pinch of baking powder, not at all unlike a proper pancake. The quantity of each will depend on the consistency of your ingredients (potatoes require less flour than beans would, for example), but ultimately you're looking for a slightly thick batter. Make sure all of your ingredients are room temperature so that they will blend well and you won't end up cooking your eggs with hot ingredients. If the batter seems too thick, add another egg, if it's too thin, add more flour. When you're moderately happy with it, fry one up in some melted butter or cook it on a griddle and then give it a taste. You may need to adjust the consistency or the seasonings before cooking up the rest of the batter.

It may require a bit of kitchen play, but that's what cooking should really be about. Use a recipe as a jumping-off point for your own creative urges. Don't be afraid to dabble in the spice cabinet or toss in some herbs. If you don't like what you've created, the worst thing that could happen is you end up tossing leftovers that more than likely would've found their way to the rubbish bin before too long anyway.

Corn and Crawfish Flitters

I made these for Media Night at the Food Network during the Next Food Network Star competition and people really enjoyed them. By the end of the night, I'd said the word "flitters" so many times that it started sounding pretty silly to me. I guess it still does!

½ - 1 cup whole wheat, all purpose flour
2 Eggs, beaten
¾ cup Crawfish Tail Meat
Fresh corn kernels from 1 ear, sliced from the cob
¼ teaspoon cayenne pepper
¼ teaspoon cumin, ground
Salt/Pepper
Fresh Cilantro

In a skillet on high heat, sear the corn until the edges just start to caramelize. Season with cayenne, salt, pepper, and cumin to taste and let the corn cool. Add the crawfish meat and cooled corn in a mixing bowl and combine with eggs and fresh cilantro. Add just enough flour to make a batter the consistency of pancake batter. Pour batter into a hot skillet with just enough clarified butter to cover the bottom of the pan. Cook flitters on both sides until golden brown. Drain flitters on paper towels and serve with sour cream.

What comes around...

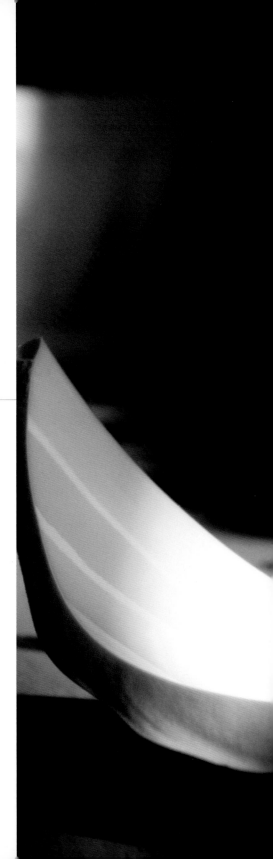

Contrary to popular belief, trash does NOT disappear when the garbage man hauls it away. It goes somewhere, and those somewheres are getting full. I'll admit that our family came to our recycling epiphany late in the game. We live in an area where recycling is not only voluntary, but inconvenient to boot. Around here, people would just as soon throw it away than sort it, load it, and haul it to the not-so-nearby recycling center where you then have to unload it and distribute it to the various receptacles. So when we decided as a family to begin our recycling efforts, the process was cumbersome and altogether laborious. But now we're recycling fiends! It gets in your blood and you find yourself taking home plastic drink containers to recycle them rather than simply tossing them in a convenient trashcan. We recycle everything we can, from cardboard and paper to metals and plastic. Not only do we feel good about what we recycle, we're making better decisions about what foods we buy and how they're packaged. We're bringing our own shopping bags to the market (we use those giant blue IKEA bags for nearly everything) and avoiding packaging with unnecessary layers of plastic. And if you can't recycle it, find some interesting way to reuse it; a broken bowl is reborn in a mosaic, an old bowling ball becomes garden art. Are we enviro-nuts? We're not extreme, but we are conscious and that feels right.

Recycling also applies to vegetative matter. My father started a compost heap at the Inn when I was just a boy and it's been the local worms' favorite hangout ever since. People are always commenting on how nice the grounds look at the Inn, the geraniums bright-red; the hanging baskets overflowing. My Dad's always quick to point out that he composts. I remember one time we had a part-time waitress who wanted to know why we didn't just use dirt. As silly as the question seemed at the time, you'll be amazed how many people don't understand what compost is and how its nutrient-laden bulk is like pure gold for the garden. Of course if you don't have a yard, composting may be out of the question. But if you do, consider devoting a tiny portion of it for creating a composting area. Your plants will thank you for it.

Kohl-what?

One of the greatest things about food and the preparation of food is that you never stop learning. Just when you think you have a handle on your basic kitchen knowledge you stumble across an unusual root or fruit or spice and immediately you're exposed to a whole new world of possibilities. For some, these "new" ingredients may simply be variables in a dull equation. For me, they're shiny new toys in my toy box and I can't wait to bring those new finds back to the kitchen. Having been raised in a restaurant I sometimes take for granted what may seem like unusual fare to most. I find that what's commonplace to me may be completely alien to others and I love introducing people to new tastes and textures.

One of the most overlooked members of the Brassica family (which includes cabbage, Brussels sprouts, cauliflower and broccoli to name a few) is the odd-looking kohlrabi. The plant sports a large, solid sphere at its base that's topped with tall leafy greens. Depending on the cultivar, the bulb can range in color form a light, frosty green all the way to a deep Concord purple. No matter what the exterior color, the interior flesh of the kohlrabi bulb is a pale to creamy white. Larger bulbs can tend to be somewhat tough or woody, so look for specimens that are about the size of a tennis or baseball. The greens are edible (and delicious), so try and select kohlrabi with vibrant, healthy greens on top. It's being grown by more and more local farms, so there's a good chance you'll find it at your local farmers' market if you get there early enough.

Kohlrabi has been cultivated in central Europe for centuries but is just now becoming popular in the States. The name kohlrabi comes from the German word kohl, meaning cabbage, and rabi, meaning turnip, which pretty much accurately describes the vegetable. Eaten raw, kohlrabi is reminiscent of crunchy broccoli stems with a touch of radish. To enjoy it raw, simply peel the bulb and grate or slice it. It's excellent tossed into a fresh salad or served with a selection of mixed crudités. When cooked the flesh loses a bit of its radish bite and tastes more like fresh cooked cabbage. In Europe it's often cooked with cream or sour cream and seasoned simply with salt, pepper and perhaps a squeeze of lemon or a dash of vinegar.

The next time you're perusing the produce department, keep your eyes peeled for kohlrabi and give it a try. In fact, look for anything unusual and let me know what you find. I'm always keen to learn something new.

Kohlrabi with Sour Cream

4 medium kohlrabi bulbs
1 tablespoon butter
1 tablespoon olive oil
1 garlic clove; finely chopped
1 medium Onion; chopped
1 tablespoon Lemon juice
2 tablespoon fresh parsley; chopped
Salt & freshly ground pepper
2 tablespoon sour cream
nutmeg

Peel the tough outer skin from the kohlrabi, then cut
the bulbs into large matchsticks. In a skillet, heat butter
and olive oil. Add garlic, onion and kohlrabi and sauté,
stirring for 5 to 7 minutes until kohlrabi is tender crisp.
Stir in lemon juice and parsley, then season with salt,
pepper and nutmeg to taste. Stir in sour cream, and
serve hot.

Return of the Cave Carrots

Ingredients are a bit like fashion. Who knows what triggers it, but if you pay attention, you'll notice certain foods suddenly popping up everywhere and then, for no apparent reason, they seem to vanish. Take parsnips for example. There was a time when parsnips were far more popular than their carrot cousins, when you'd find them tucked into pot pies or roasted and smashed next to a piece of baked chicken. I'm proud to see that these deliciously sweet, pale taproots are making a slow, but steady comeback.

My personal parsnip obsession began about a decade ago and in much the same way most of my food crushes happen. Like some spelunker in a cave, I treat trips to the market more like an expedition than a mere shopping chore. I'd heard of parsnips, but had no idea what to do with them. I'm drawn to new or forgotten ingredients like a weasel to a henhouse.

Because of their pale flesh, my friend Richard refers to parsnips as Cave Carrots and it's a name that's stayed with me. They do, in fact, look like carrots that have been starved of light, developing over time into albino versions of their orangy kin. The truth is, parsnips are more closely related to parsley than to carrots and are sometimes mistakenly sold as parsley root (which do resemble parsnips but are generally smaller and thinner). Parsnips only develop their unique, earthy sweetness after they've been exposed to cold weather, so while the roots mature in the relentless heat of the summer months, they aren't harvested until the ground turns cold, forcing the plant to store its sugars down into its main tap root. While you can certainly eat them raw, I believe their magic isn't truly unlocked until they're cooked.

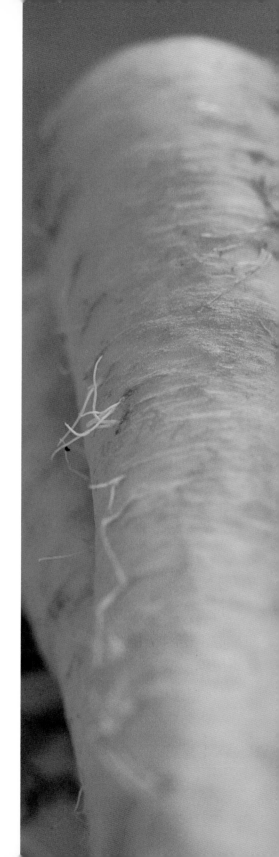

Honey-Lavender Roasted Parsnips

My family's favorite way to enjoy parsnips is to simply roast them tossed in a simple mixture of honey, a little oil and my Out of the Blue salt. The lavender from the Out of the Blue salt perfumes the whole house as the sweet parsnips inhale that floral magic. There's no real recipe here … just toss your peeled and roughly chopped parsnips with a couple tablespoons of good, local honey, a good shake of Out of the Blue salt (or just sea salt), and a light drizzle of avocado or olive oil. We usually spread them out on a parchment paper lined cookie sheet. Roast in the oven at 400° F degrees until the parsnips become knife tender. Depending on the thickness of the parsnips, this could be anywhere from 15-30 minutes, but just check them from time to time. And when you're checking, just give the pan a good shake to make sure everything gets well nice and tossed around. These make an excellent side, or even as part of nice winter salad.

Parsnip, Apple, and Celeriac Soup

This somewhat German inspired concoction partners parsnips with crisp apples and celeriac (celery root), a delightful soup that makes a solid addition to any autumn menu. Enjoy!

6 cups vegetable stock
4-5 local apples peeled & cut into 1" cubes (Johnna Gold, Mutzu, or Granny Smith work well here)
2 large parsnips peeled and cut into 1" cubes
1 small celeriac (celery root) peeled and cut into 1" cubes
2 tablespoon olive oil
2 tablespoon butter
½ cup sour cream
¼ cup Calvados (or good quality Apple Brandy)
Salt to taste
¼ teaspoon white pepper
¼ teaspoon freshly grated nutmeg

Sauté apples, parsnips, and celeriac in olive oil, butter, and calvados on medium-high heat until just slightly golden. Season with nutmeg, salt, and white pepper. Add vegetable stock and simmer until vegetables are just soft. Add sour cream and puree with an immersion blender or food processor until the soup is as smooth or chunky as you like. If the soup is too thick, simply add more stock. Garnish with a little dollop of sour cream, a little more grated nutmeg, and a sprig of fresh herbs.

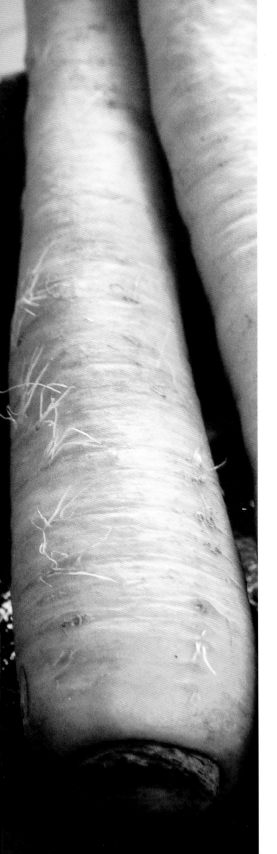

Parsnips have a reputation of being somewhat woody and fibrous, and truth be told, they can be. The trick is to cook them until they are meltingly soft and once they've passed that threshold, those stringy fibers completely disappear, giving way to buttery soft flesh, much the way the flesh of hard winter squash transforms when cooked. You can use parsnips in any recipe that calls for carrots, potatoes, or other root veggies like rutabagas or turnips. We eat them all the time and I think once you try them, you will too.

Eating Raw

Over the last few thousand years, food has become an inseparable part of our culture, a defining and glorious element of what makes life enjoyable. While our minds may revel on a food's taste, to our body, it's all just fuel. With instances of diabetes, high cholesterol, and high blood pressure on the rise, the correlation between what we eat and how we feel has never been more clear.

Remember that whole food pyramid thing your teacher talked about in school? The concept of eating a balanced diet came about when scientists began to truly understand how food is broken down on a cellular level and what our cells need to stay healthy. But before our cells can absorb the fuel locked inside our food, it has to be broken down. That's where enzymes come into play.

Raw foods like fruits and vegetables naturally contain the enzymes needed to break those foods down in our bodies. Most raw foods are alive with enzymes that are crucial to not only healthy digestion, but healthy living. Once raw foods are exposed to temperatures above 118 degrees, however, those crucial enzymes are destroyed. Since those natural enzymes are now missing, our bodies must utilize valuable metabolic enzymes to help digest the cooked food. Have you ever felt tired or sluggish after a big meal? That's because our bodies must burn energy to manufacture those enzymes. Some studies even suggest that the ingestion of too many cooked foods can be detrimental to our immune systems. In general, raw food is more easily digested, passing through the digestive tract in about half the time it takes for cooked food to make the same journey.

So am I suggesting you stop cooking? Absolutely not. What I am suggesting is that you try to incorporate more raw fruits and vegetables into your diet. Be aware of the life that lies within our foods, and how those essential digestive enzymes can not only aide in digestion, but effect your health overall. Start by trying to incorporate at least one raw food every meal … a little side salad, fresh relish, or even some slices of fruit. Your body will thank you for it.

Fresh Beet Relish

Here's a beautiful red, sweet-hot relish that would be wonderful served with a nice grilled pork chop or even a broiled piece of fish. The heat comes from the fresh grated horseradish root, so if you want less heat, cut back on the horseradish. Enjoy!

Combine
1 firm apple, cored, peeled, and grated
1 medium beet, peeled and grated
2 teaspoon honey (preferably local)
2 teaspoon cider vinegar
1-3 teaspoons fresh grated horseradish (as you like)
¼ cup golden raisins
pinch of salt

Sprout!

One of the easiest ways to incorporate some raw food elements into your diet is by eating sprouts. Sprouts are powerhouses if nutrients and enzymes, and they're fun to grow too! All you need is an old-fashioned mason jar, a screen lid (available on-line, or if you're crafty, you can make one yourself), and a sunny window sill. Every day, just fill the jar with lukewarm water, swish it around, then drain the jar. Do this 2 or 3 times a day until the sprouts are alive and fluffy. If your kids turn their noses up to anything green, let them grow their own sprouts. As the seedlings grow, so does the children's excitement and before you know it, they'll be shoveling the tiny greens into their mouths with glee.

Our Children's Palates

It's no secret that, as far as food is concerned, my sister Sonja and I were spoiled. When our bellies rumbled, we'd simply descend the twelve-and-a-half steps that separated our home from our restaurant. One night it would be French onion soup and grouper Grenoble style, the next night ... well, it would be grouper Grenoble style and French onion soup. For us, "gourmet" food was commonplace ... even boring. We'd eaten the whole menu again and again and again. I would go through cycles, eating the same thing night after tongue-numbing night for weeks on end. I probably had French onion soup every night of my life from age 12 to 16. On a few occasions, to escape the doldrums of fine dining, I'd hop on my bike and ride about two miles to the Jasper Dairy Queen. Fast food was a treat, a strange vacation from the culinary norm.

But despite my early fast food treasons, it unnerves me to see a burger unwrapped on the table at a Chinese restaurant or even French fries on the menu of the local Mexican joint. At the Inn we'd have parents that would swear their kids would only eat burgers or pizza. My dad would make it a point to convince (or perhaps, more accurately, trick) stubborn children and their passive parents that they would enjoy Wiener Schnitzel, Chicken Parmesan, or even a bit of flounder (cut into fish sticks, of course). With a bit of effort and just a dash of cooperation from the parents, the kids would always come away from the table excited, basking in their parents' praise.

But the question really is, why all the fuss? What happened that turned kids into fast food zombies? Why is it that kids in other parts of the world eat damn near anything and our kids only eat junk? The answer is obvious: it's the parents' fault! Our taste buds mature as we do, but ONLY if they're trained. It's our job as parents to expose our kids to real food. You'll still end up at the drive-thru from time to time, but don't let those occasions define their life's menu.

Of course, young or old, we each have our own individual and inexplicable tastes. My son Finn has loved black olives since he was a baby, so we assumed that Ella would love them as well. Wrong. Ella could literally drink Balsamic vinegar and asks for it nearly every meal. Finn can't stand it. There are things that your kids simply won't like. But when you involve your kids with food by taking them to the farmers' markets, planting herbs or veggies at home, or letting them lend a simple hand in the kitchen, you'll find that their list of 'likes' is much longer than their list of 'dislikes'.

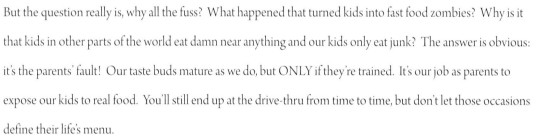

Rocky Road

Nothing lights up kids' little eyes like chocolate!
When my wife brings out the chocolate, it's a race to
the kitchen. Of course we're not quite brave enough to
tackle anything fancy, but something simple like Rocky
Road is a great project for kids.

Chocolate can be a little finicky if you don't know
what you're doing. Heat it too quickly and the fat will
actually separate from the cocoa, leaving you with
a sticky, oily mess. Cook it too long and it'll scorch,
a kitchen nightmare that you'll never forget. The
trick is to melt the chocolate over slow, steady heat.
This process is called tempering, and it's an essential
part of working with chocolate. One of the easiest
ways to temper chocolate is to use a double boiler
(sometimes called a bain-marie). Simply take a pot
and add a couple inches of water and bring it to a low
boil. Put your chocolate into a heat-proof bowl and set
it over the steaming pot. The steam gently melts the
chocolate without the risk of separation or burning.

Here's how we make our Rocky Road:

12 oz. milk chocolate chips
6 oz. bittersweet chocolate chips
½ cup Brazil nuts
⅔ cup mini-marshmallows

Using the method described above, temper the
chocolates, stirring gently to combine. Remove
from the heat and immediately stir in the nuts and
marshmallows. While the mixture is still warm, pour
into small baking cups or simply make small islands on
a sheet of waxed paper. Refrigerate until firm then try
and keep the kids away! Feel free to substitute Brazil
nuts for your favorite nut or mix in other ingredients
like dried fruit, coconut or candy pieces.

The Hunt for the Golden Mushroom

One of my early childhood food inhibitions involved mushrooms. If you were to ask me, I'd swear to the end of the earth that I hated them and would sooner eat a live newt than pop a piece of that fungus in my mouth. I'd had a bad run-in with a can of Cream of Mushroom soup* that left me covered in itchy hives, so I liked to pull the "I'm allergic to them" excuse when the M word was spoken. Besides, canned mushrooms in any form are, let's be honest, nothing like their fresh counterparts. So when my father offered to take me hunting for the golden Chanterelle mushrooms that sometimes appear in the mountains that surround the Inn, I almost refused. But somehow he convinced me to go (looking back, I'm not sure I had an option!) and we had a great time. It was like a giant Easter egg hunt, but without the whole mythical rabbit business. Not only did we fill our baskets with mushrooms, but we came away with all sorts of garden treasures like acorns, unique leaves and rocks, and even a molted crawfish shell. Later that afternoon, when the smell of those sautéing chanterelles entered my room, I instantly became a mushroom lover. I knew I'd smelled that aroma before, but these were MY mushrooms picked that magical afternoon in the shadow of the Appalachians.

As soon as my children were old enough to hold their own basket, their Opa (my father) and I introduced the joy of mushroom hunting to the next generation of Ruefferts. And just like their father, my kids were heavy with anticipation at first. Now they're the ones asking me when we can head to the mountains to look for those magnificent golden mushrooms … plus whatever else we may find.

*Author's note- Since I was old enough to read the labels on those red and white cans of soup, I've always been confused by the term "Cream of." Cream of mushroom? That's not even physiologically possible is it? Can you milk a mushroom? Or a stalk of celery? And can you imagine the look on a hen's face if you tried to extract some dairy product from its mammary-less body? Wouldn't "Creamy Mushroom Soup" sound a little better? Maybe I'm over thinking this …

The Land of the Midnight Sun

The road trip from my Uncle Wolfgang's house in Emden, Germany to his summer getaway in Sør Trondelag, Norway seemed endless. We took the ferry from Kiel to Oslo then headed north toward the Trondheim Fjord. The countless miles gave me ample time to wonder what I'd gotten myself into: seven weeks in Norway with no electricity, no running water, and perhaps more importantly, no Atari. When my father and my Uncle suggested I take the trip, I accepted without giving any thought to the realities of the journey. I didn't know that I'd have to leave my mother sobbing at the airport and I never thought my 9-year-old eyes would cry until I was halfway across the Atlantic (for the record, I didn't start crying until she did). I spent much of that drive thinking of all the reasons why I shouldn't be there, completely ignoring the spectacular Norwegian countryside until it was time to stop and vomit on it ... English peas and After Eights from the ferry. Ugh. Perhaps my carsick brain was trying to make me pay a little more attention to what is arguably one of Mother Nature's finest landscapes.

We'd seen glimpses of the sea as we traveled, but it wasn't until we arrived at the farm of Lars Løvbugt (RIP) that I fully began to appreciate the majesty of the fjords. Lars was the quintessential Norwegian, part farmer, part fisherman with hands like leather and deep weathered lines around his eyes. Uncle Wolfgang had befriended Lars some years earlier and kept a small cottage at the bottom of his property and a boat just off shore. Before we unpacked the VW van, we walked down to the steep rocks that bordered the cold, dark water. I vaguely remembered being warned that the rocks were slippery as I fell into the icy sea. I still recall how clean the saltwater tasted as I pulled myself back onto those rocks. My Tante (aunt) Putzi would later use that same clean seawater to make Saltzkartoffeln (salt potatoes) that were so good we'd eat them later as a snack, cold with just a smear of mayonnaise.

Pannekaken
(Whole Wheat Crepes)

The only thing better than pancakes are waffles, and this recipe will make those too! I like these with a dollop of homemade preserves and some cottage cheese or with soft butter and maple syrup.

2 large eggs
1 cup milk
⅓ cup water
1 cup whole wheat flour
¼ teaspoon salt
2 tablespoons butter, melted

In a blender or food processor, blend the eggs, milk, water, flour, salt, and the 2 tablespoons melted butter for 5 seconds, or until smooth. Refrigerate batter for at least 30 minutes (batter can be made up to a day in advance). Place a lightly buttered crepe pan on medium heat, pour about 3 tablespoons of the batter in the pan, swirling the pan to evenly distribute the batter. When the crepe sets, gently turn out onto a plate or wax paper. Repeat until all the batter is used. Extra crepes can be frozen and reheated for future use.

Beet and Herring Salad
with Apples

Sweet, sour, crunchy and smooth.
I can eat this stuff all day!

2 large beets
8 oz. Pickled Herring in wine
4 shallots, peeled and thinly sliced
2 Granny Smith apples
2 tablespoons white vinegar (if needed)

Boil beets until they're knife tender. Remove the beets and drop them into ice water until they're well cooled. Drain and peel the beets using a paper towel to rub off the skins. Cut them in half then slice them into 1/8th inch slices. Drain the herring, then toss together the shallots, herring, sliced beets, and apples. Some herring are more sour than others, so the vinegar may or may not be needed.

Pressed Cucumber Salad

This easy side goes great with hot or cold foods. If you're not a fan of sour cream, try it with some plain yogurt.

2 large European seedless cucumbers
1 tablespoon sea salt
3 tablespoons fresh dill, chopped
¼ cup sour cream (organic is best)
1 tablespoon white vinegar

Peel cucumbers and slice as thin as you can, using a mandolin if you have one. Add salt to cucumbers and place in a wide colander. Place colander over another bowl and place weights on top of cucumbers (plates work fine). Place the whole mess in the fridge and let drain for at least 30 minutes. Once the cukes have drained, toss in the vinegar, sour cream, and fresh dill.

Caraway Cabbage

Some folks like to cook cabbage until the whole neighborhood smells like the stuff, but a quick sauté keeps it sweet and crunchy. Traditionally white cabbage is used, but red cabbage, Nappa or a combination of different varieties works nicely here too.

1 small head cabbage (3 cups)
1 chopped sweet yellow onion (½ cup)
½ stick butter
2 teaspoons caraway seeds
½ teaspoon salt
½ teaspoon fresh ground white pepper
Parsley, coarse chopped

In a large skillet, melt the butter over medium heat. Add the onion, cabbage and caraway seeds. Sauté and stir over medium heat until the cabbage is just tender. Toss in parsley and transfer to a medium serving bowl.

Though I certainly didn't realize it then, my time in Norway was a culinary awakening for me. For seven weeks, we literally lived off of the land and sea. With the exception of a few staple items (bread, butter, mayonnaise, etc.), we ate what we harvested: fish and shellfish from the ocean, berries and mushrooms from the forests surrounding the fjord. In the early morning we'd pull in the nets filled with herring for Lars to salt or pickle. For breakfast we'd eat lumpfish roe on toast and soft boiled eggs. By mid-morning we were catching mackerel or coalfish for Wolfgang to smoke or for Putzi to fry. After lunch, we'd forage the woods for the yolk-yellow Chanterelle mushrooms which would end up simply prepared with bacon and scrambled eggs. Or we'd search for the wild blueberries, raspberries, and cloudberries that we'd later eat with vanilla sauce. In the evening we'd pull in the traps to find stone crabs and lobsters that were simply eaten cold on buttered bread. Sleep doesn't come easy in the land of the Midnight Sun (the first night of which is called Saint Hans day) and we'd whittle away the bright nights playing cards and eating crawfish salad on toast; a snooze-less meal between dinner and breakfast.

I returned to Norway in 1999 with my father, half expecting the magic of those memories to tarnish in the reality of time. If anything, that return visit only reinforced the startling beauty and charm of Norway, reconnecting me with the sea that I both admired and feared as a child. It's amazing how food can connect us to a place, remind us of how inseparably linked our past is with our present. Those salty weeks in the Trondheim Fjord were an awakening for me, a set of vivid, indelible memories that opened a young boy's eyes forever.

Saltzkartoffeln (Salt Potatoes)

This is my family's favorite way to eat potatoes, especially when the dish you're serving them with has some type of sauce or gravy. They come out of the pot all broken and fluffy around the edges. Save any leftovers for a quick potato salad or a simple midnight snack with mayo.

3 large baking potatoes, peeled
3 tablespoons coarse sea salt
water

These are easy and fantastic. Cut peeled potatoes into large chunks and place in a large pan with well fitting lid. Add just enough water to cover the potatoes and add the salt. You want the water to taste like the ocean. Boil uncovered until the potatoes are just knife tender. Drain away salt water and put the lid on the pot. Hold the lid tightly in place and vigorously shake the pot about 5-6 times. Remove the lid and cover the pan with a towel until ready to serve.

Sour Cream & Raisin Pie

I know some of you are turning your noses up at the idea of sour cream and raisins, but you're just going to have to trust me here. I like this served cold with a warm, frothy latte to wash it all down.

1 cup sour cream
1 cup white sugar
2 eggs, beaten
1 teaspoon baking powder
1 pinch salt
1 teaspoon cinnamon
½ teaspoon nutmeg
½ teaspoon ground cloves
2 tablespoons white vinegar
1 cup raisins
1 unbaked 9 inch pie crust

Preheat oven to 350° degrees F.
In a medium bowl, stir together sour cream and sugar until smooth and creamy. Stir in eggs, baking powder, salt, cinnamon, nutmeg, cloves, vinegar, and raisins; mix until well blended. Pour mixture into pie crust. Bake in a preheated oven 40 to 50 minutes until just set. Cool in refrigerator 2 hours before serving. Garnish with fresh sliced apples or pears.

Dorsk mit Tomatsmor
(Pan sautéed Cod with Tomato Butter)

When most people think of cod, they think of frozen fish sticks. What a waste of cod! Buy a piece of fresh cod and you'll be amazed. It's moist, buttery, firm, flaky and all around delicious.

For the Tomato Butter:

8 tablespoons unsalted butter - softened
2 tablespoons concentrated tomato paste
2 tablespoons finely chopped dill
¼ teaspoon sea salt
¼ teaspoon white pepper

Combine all ingredients in a mixing bowl and mix well. Place prepared butter in a small bowl and refrigerate for up to 3 days. Butter can also be frozen for 2 to 3 weeks. Defrost in refrigerator. Bring to room temperature before using.

For the fish:

6 oz. Cod Filet (per person)
salt/white pepper
¼ cup flour
3 tablespoons butter
1 tablespoon olive oil

Cod is a gorgeous, flaky-fleshed fish that's often overlooked for inferior fish with flashier names. It's a no-brainer that's sure to impress. Season each fillet with salt and white pepper, then dust top and bottom with flour. Melt butter in an ovenproof skillet over medium-high heat and add olive oil. When butter/oil mixture is hot, add cod and cook about 3 minutes on each side. Fish is done when a knife inserted feels little to no resistance. Serve with tomato dill butter and a slice of lemon.

When Food Sings

Cooking for me has always been playtime … a time to experiment, a time to create. A trip to a decent market can literally leave me mentally exhausted after thinking about all of the potential flavor and texture combinations that cram each and every aisle. I try not to go to the market hungry, knowing full well that I'll end up buying more than I could ever hope to prepare before the ingredients expire. The hardest part can be trying to exercise some restraint in those markets, taking away only what you need.

Restraint in the kitchen can be tough as well. Knowing what NOT to add to a dish is as important as what TO add. Certain food combinations inherently work better than others and most of us have a basic feel for what works well with what. When you work with food professionally, you're always looking to push those familiar tastes just a little. It's exciting! Sometimes those experiments end up in the trashcan, but I believe you can learn as much from a bad meal as you can from a great one. Other times, the food just sings. A harmonious chord is struck, aligning flavor, texture, color, and imaginative spark. Those culinary epiphanies keep me coming back to the kitchen again and again.

I'm often asked "What's your favorite dish to cook?" and I usually have a hard time conjuring up an answer. The truth is, it changes. I think all good cooks are somewhat attention deficit by nature. Once we're created something fun and tasty, we're off on some other thread to create the next fun and tasty thing. As you discover new ingredients, you become somewhat infatuated with them, incorporating them into dishes for the sheer sake of trying.

So don't be afraid to experiment. The worst thing that can happen is that you eat a lackluster meal, but it'll be a lackluster meal that you'll remember and will never recreate.

Apples

I grew up (and still live) in the shadow of Georgia's apple capital, where gnarled and twisted apple trees line the rolling hills of Gilmer and Fannin counties. To be honest, I always took them for granted. I just assumed that all apples were crisp, tart and delicious until I had the opportunity to do some traveling and discover that not all apples are created equal. Like many of the fruits and vegetable you'll find in your average grocer, most modern apple varieties have been hybridized to be large, beautiful, and bruise-resistant. Of course those are great qualities to have, but not if you sacrifice the flavor and texture of the apple. When you visit an old-fashioned apple orchard, you'll be amazed at both the quality and variety of fruits they have to offer. The skin might not shine like they've been lacquered with polyurethane and you might find a blemish or two, but once you bite into an honest-to-goodness apple, you'll probably never go back to those over-bred grocery store varieties. The best part is, apples are grown in almost every state in the country and an increasing number of specialty grocers are starting to showcase more old-fashioned, un-shiny apples. An apple a day might not keep the doctor away, but it will make you smile …

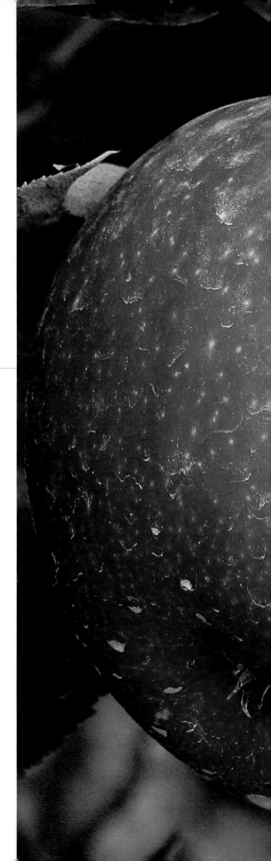

Spanish Mackerel
with Apple-Corn Relish

Mackerel isn't one of the most popular fish at the market but, in my opinion, it should be. It's loaded with cancer fighting Omega-3s and holds up wonderfully grilled, baked, seared, broiled and even fried. The combination of sweet apples and sweet, fresh corn really sing in this dish, adding a crisp texture to the buttery fish. Add sweet crabmeat to the equation and before long, you'll be saying: Holy Mackerel!

2 boneless Spanish mackerel fillets (6-8 oz. each)
¼ teaspoon whole grain mustard
¼ teaspoon dill
¼ teaspoon salt
¼ teaspoon pepper
½ tablespoon oil
2 slices bacon, chopped
¼ cup red onion, diced
3 Gala apples; peeled, cored, & chopped
2 cups fresh corn kernels
salt
1 teaspoon freshthyme leaves
1 pinch cayenne pepper
½ cup fresh crabmeat, lump or claw

Put the oil, mustard, dill, ¼ teaspoon salt and pepper on a plate. Dredge the fish in the mixture, making sure to coat both sides of each fillet. In a heavy skillet over medium-high heat, sear the fish for about 2 minutes per side.

While the fish is cooking, add bacon to a medium skillet over high heat and sauté until the bacon begins to sweat. Add the onion, apples, corn and a pinch of salt. When is heated through but still crunchy, add the thyme, cayenne pepper and crab meat. Gently toss or stir together and remove from the heat.

To serve, simply top each fillet with a generous portion of the Apple-Corn Relish and garnish with a little more fresh thyme. Holy Mackerel ... oh wait ... I've already used that line.

Apple Strudel

This is an easy version of apple strudel, not one meant to rival those you'll find in Germany or Austria. But let's be honest, you wouldn't make it as often if you had to go through all that trouble making dough from scratch, right? So keep it simple and cook!

3 Jona Gold apples
1 Jona Gold apple, shredded & covered with lemon juice
2 tablespoon apple butter
½ cup pecans or sliced almonds
½ cup prunes
¼ cup brown sugar
1 tablespoon Sugar Baby (or cinnamon sugar)
1 sheet puff pastry, thawed
1 egg
¼ cup milk

Preheat your oven to 375° F. Beat the egg and milk together with a fork and set aside for a moment. On a lightly floured or nonstick work surface, roll the puff pastry out to about one and a half times its original size.

Next, in a large bowl mix the apples, butter, pecans, prunes, and both sugars. Place the mixture in the middle of the puff pastry in an even pile stretching from left to right.. Fold over one side of pastry and brush the egg mixture on the top edge. Then gently fold the opposite edge over the first one, overlapping by at least an inch or so. Brush a little more of the egg wash over the pastry and sprinkle a little more Sugar Baby on top. to brown in oven. Cut slits into pastry to let steam out, then bake in a 375° F oven for about 30 minutes or until golden brown. To serve, dust with powdered sugar and serve with ice cream or vanilla sauce and some fresh mint.

For a holiday variation, omit the prunes and the apple butter and add a bag of cranberries (fresh or frozen). Good stuff!

Pecans

There's an old pecan tree just down the street from the Woodbridge Inn. Fat black crows were always the first to enjoy the nuts, their strong beaks peeling away the leathery husk and then cracking the tiger-marked shells with relative ease. The tree's far-reaching branches have been shading Birch Street since I was a little boy, my bicycle wheels crushing the empty, discarded nut shells like popcorn as I rode my bike in the Fall. For weeks, the crows would gorge themselves on the nuts until it seemed like there would benone left for my father, who walked beneath the branches while making mental calculations each day, wondering what his take would be. The tree wasn't on our property, but the folks who had planted it nearly half a century earlier were old and didn't seem to mind the birds, or my father, pilfering the fallen nuts from their front lawn and the street. When the property became available my father quickly purchased it, more for the tree than for the house, I believe. The crows still visit each year, and I can't say that I blame them.

Georgia grows more pecans than just about anyone, and no Southern home is complete without an old pecan tree in the yard. As you drive through the southern states, you'll see mile after mile of old pecan plantations. They've become a symbol of the South, solid with deep roots in history. In the kitchen, pecans are excellent in both sweet and savory applications and they're full of protein. While they are a little high in fat, it's the "good" unsaturated fat that helps reduce LDL cholesterol levels in the blood. On top of that, they're absolutely delicious. So keep your eyes on the pecan trees and when the crows start to look fat, you'll know it's almost your turn to enjoy the South's favorite nut.

Ginger-Cream Pecan Pie

Freshly grated ginger adds a little punch to this Southern classic. There are literally hundreds of pecan pie variations out there, but I think this one really stands out. If you're good at making your own pastry crust and you have the time, then go for it.

¼ cup half & half
½ cup maple syrup
½ cup brown sugar
3 eggs
½ teaspoon freshly grated ginger
2 tablespoon melted butter
1 cup pecans, chopped
1 ready-made frozen piecrust, thawed

Preheat oven to 325° F. Gently press the piecrust into a glass or ceramic pie plate.

Whisk half & half, syrup, sugar, eggs, ginger and butter together until well blended. Stir in the pecans and pour the mix into crust. Bake for 40 – 45 minutes until the whole thing is golden brown and irresistible.

Spiced Pecans

Don't be surprised if these incredibly tasty treats disappear before your very eyes. Crumble them over salads or roasted winter squash, or just eat them as an unforgettable snack.

4 cups pecans, toasted 8-10 minutes
1 tablespoon melted butter
1 tablespoon brown sugar
salt
½ teaspoon curry powder
½ tablespoon pumpkin seed oil

Add all the ingredients to a large bowl and simply toss them together, making sure each nut is well coated. Place on a Silpat parchment paper-lined baking tray and bake for 3 – 5 minutes in a 325° F oven. Pecans burn easily, so make sure to keep an eye on them. More than likely, you'll have to keep an eye on them after they come out of the oven too … they'll be gone before you know it.

Pecan Encrusted Trout with Orange-Mint Relish

The only thing better than a rainbow trout is a rainbow trout covered in pecans!

2 oranges, segmented
2 tablespoon mint, chopped
salt
¼ cup Spiced Pecans, chopped (see preceding recipe)
1 tablespoon butter
1 tablespoon oil
2 trout filets
pepper
1 cup flour
2 eggs, beaten
1 cup pecan meal or finely chopped pecans

Mix together the oranges, mint, a pinch of salt, and spiced pecans in a bowl and let sit while preparing the trout.

Place the flour, eggs, and pecan meal in three separate plates. Put the oil and butter in a large skillet over medium-high heat. Dredge the trout fillets in flour, then egg, and then pecan meal and carefully place the fish, skin side up in the hot pan. Cook the fillets for about 2 minutes per side and remove from the skillet. Top each fillet with the Orange-Mint relish and garnish with some chopped mint and crumbled Spiced Pecans.

Thin Ice, Warm Food

When I was about 10 years old, we had an unusually harsh winter here in the North Georgia mountains. The local city pond, home to catfish, tadpoles, dragonfly nymphs, and angry ducks in the summer, froze solid. There had been ice on the pond in previous years, but not like this...thick as bricks and slick as...well, slick as ice. The edges of the pond were a bit slushy, but the center seemed solid enough for my dad to take me and my sister ice skating. Sonja and Dad were seasoned skaters and had their own skates, but I just slid around in my shoes until gravity brought me down to the frozen surface again and again. Is it me or does ice have a stronger gravitational pull than other solid surfaces? Anyway, the whole town thought we were crazy when the local paper posted pictures of our ice-capades that following week. They were probably right. There was a strong chance that the ice on that murky pond would crack and we would all fall in. But the ice held and so do the memories.

In the winter months following my chemo and radiation therapies, I felt like my blood had frozen over. The 70 pounds of fat and muscle I'd lost left me with little to protect my bones from the cold. In those frigid hours my mind kept returning to that pond and I realized that living with cancer is a bit like walking on thin ice. For the rest of my life I'm going to be walking on that ice, hoping that the stuff holds solid and I avoid the cracks and faults that threaten to send me falling. My sister Sonja beat her breast cancer and then set out walking on the ice again. Ultimately, she fell through. The cancer returned and took her under. Truly, none of us can say when our ice will crack, so there's really no point in walking lightly. Run as fast as you can while you can. Run forward and run hard.

So when you're freezing to the bone and worried about the thickness of the ice, run for the kitchen and find comfort in the simple pleasures of a warm meal.

Joe Rueffert and friends try a little ice skating on a frozen pond in Jasper Tuesday morning. The -7° low left not only ponds and streams frozen, but countless water pipes all over the county, along with numerous automobiles which failed to start.

Jan 1982

Hans' Simple Homemade Chili

Nothing warms your bones or your soul like a bowl of chili on a brisk Autumn day. The mere mention of chili at my house results in wide eyes, bright smiles, and a sense of anticipation. Anticipation because chili is never the same thing twice in my kitchen. For me, it's an excuse to really get in there and play; a chance to empty jars from the fridge and clean out the pantry. Depending on my mood and the ingredients at hand, my chili could contain the last dregs of the bottled barbecue sauce, tomato ketchup, hot sauce, mustard, salsa, or even herring paste (you'd be surprised!).

I get the opportunity to judge a chili cook-off every year and it's truly inspiring how wide the chili spectrum is. From nuclear to mild, from chunky to thin, every chili is as unique as its creator. But then how do you judge which out of 40 vastly different concoctions is the best? For me, it's all about the sauce that binds it all together. The beauty of chili is how all of the ingredients (even the weird ones) come together to form a homogenous dish. If the sauce portion of the chili doesn't taste right, then neither will the meat or the beans.

Here's a simplified breakdown of our quick and easy household standard. Use this as a starting point and then drive it in your own direction. Don't be afraid to experiment with chili. It's downright hard to make bad chili.

1	lb. ground turkey, beef, chicken, or pork
1	15 oz. can red beans (drained and rinsed)
1	15 oz. can kidney beans (drained and rinsed)
1	14.5 oz. can diced tomatoes
1	teaspoon ground cumin
2	teaspoon dried oregano
1	cup tomato ketchup (I use a German curry ketchup when I have it)
2	cloves garlic, minced
1	medium onion, diced
1	teaspoon olive oil

In a large, heavy pot add olive oil and sauté garlic and onion on high heat until they turn translucent. Add cumin and oregano and sauté for another minute. Add ground meat and cook until done. Depending on the meat used, you may need to drain some of the fat before proceeding. Reduce the heat to a medium-low and add the beans, ketchup, and tomatoes. Add salt and pepper to taste. The sauce should just be liquid enough to bind all of the ingredients. Depending on the meat used, you may need to add more ketchup. From here, it's all about your personal taste. Add powdered chilies, brown sugar, barbecue sauce, spicy mustard … or whatever! There's nothing spicy in this base recipe, so if you like it fiery, it's up to you to add that heat. Serve your chili on a pile of steamed white rice and you're ready to stare Jack Frost in the face and smile.

Gingered Carrot Bisque

As simple as this soup is, I've probably had more requests for this recipe than any other. When I was the chef at the Woodbridge Inn, I jokingly called it my "little old lady" soup because all of my surrogate grandmothers would ask me every Sunday if I'd made their favorite soup. Of course I had them all believing that I was making it just for them. You want just enough salt to bring out the sweetness of the carrot, so go easy. This soup is delicious hot or cold.

1 pound carrots, peeled and rough chopped
1 tablespoon grated ginger
2-3 cups vegetable or chicken stock
1 teaspoon ground coriander
1 teaspoon ground turmeric
1 tablespoon organic yogurt (optional)
salt to taste

In a heavy pot with tight fitting lid, steam the carrots in 1 cup of the stock for about 12 minutes or until the carrots are tender. Add the ginger, coriander, and turmeric and, using a food processor or an immersion blender, puree the carrots until velvety smooth, adding additional stock as needed to reach a thick, soupy consistency. Adjust seasoning to your liking and garnish with a dollop of yogurt or sour cream.

Cancer Wellness

I was at a Rotary Club meeting one time and a representative from the American Cancer Society was on hand to generate some interest in the local Relay for Life event. Instead of bombarding the audience with blind statistics about the disease, she did something a little more powerful.

"How many people in this room have been diagnosed with cancer?"
About three or four hands (including one of my own) were raised.
"Now, raise your hand if a family member has had cancer?"
At least half of the attendees raised their hands.
"And now, how many of you have friends that have had cancer."
As you can imagine, everyone raised a hand.

It was a simple, but powerful way to illustrate that cancer touches us all. For years, cancer has been a taboo subject. Cancer patients can often feel hopeless, powerless, rejected, frightened, confused and lonely. While they might be disease-free, the caregivers and family members have equally difficult challenges to overcome. I think my diagnosis was harder on my wife than it was for me, and she suffers mentally when I'm suffering physically.

Given that cancer touches so many of us, it's vitally important that we support everyone who's in the shadow of the disease, both patient and families alike. Fortunately, many healthcare organizations are beginning to understand the importance of support and are implementing cancer wellness programs. It may be as simple as providing a space for survivors and patients to gather and talk, but no matter how elaborate the program, it's clear that whole body wellness is in high demand.

I'm proud to be a part of the Cancer Wellness Center at Piedmont Hospital in Atlanta. In addition to meeting spaces, the Center has an amazing kitchen at its heart and I was drawn to it like a moth to a flame when I first entered the facility. Carolyn Helmer, the center's director, is a forward thinking, ultra-compassionate person who gives the center its soul and welcomes each visitor with open arms. Carolyn and I hit it off famously and I've been teaching healthy cooking demonstrations regularly ever since. The classes are for everyone under that cancer umbrella: patients, friends, family… even small children. I've fought my cancer battles and I remember them well. Radiation and chemotherapy were miserable and food was often tough to think about. But if I would've had something like the Cancer Wellness Center available to me during that time, I know my challenges would've been easier to manage. There are all sorts of classes and events that are held each month to promote mental and physical well-being, from art classes to guided imagery. It's also a wonderful research resource and a great place to talk with other patients and survivors.

Now you may not be lucky enough to get to the Piedmont Cancer Wellness Center, but I'm sure there's something similar happening in your area. And if there's not, see if you can make it happen. You may not be a cancer patient, but I guarantee there's something you could offer that would make a world of difference to a person who could use a little more support … teach a class, volunteer, or just go and talk. A little goes a long way…

The Holidays…

There is absolutely nothing more important in life than your family. As simple as that sounds, that idea was a relatively recent epiphany for me. I grew up working with my family in a high-stress environment and the holidays always meant even more stress. In the restaurant business, we work when others celebrate. If you think cooking Thanksgiving or Christmas dinner for your family is nerve racking, try doing that for 200 people who all want to eat at the same time. So I think it's fair to say that when we were all living and working together, the holidays were the time of year that we all got on each other's nerves. Don't get me wrong, we had our share of wonderful family meals, but they weren't during the holidays!

I had my first glimpse of a true family Thanksgiving when I travelled with Amy to visit her Grandma Grace and family near Statesboro, Ga. I can't really remember how I managed to get the day off from the restaurant, but I do remember the meal perfectly. It wasn't a meal, it was a feast! It took two tables, the stovetop, and every inch of counter space to display all of the food. In addition to your typical roast turkey, there were blue crabs and venison, pork roasts and ham. Pots overflowed with crowder peas, rice, green beans, creamed corn, sweet potatoes, collard greens, creamed spinach, and a rich giblet gravy studded with chopped hard-boiled eggs. We spent the entire day talking with our mouths full, revisiting the "buffet" in the late afternoon to try it all again at room temperature.

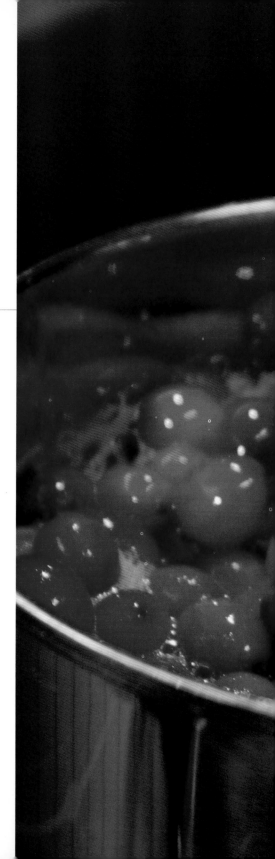

The holidays are a great excuse to put on a real spread, to roll up your sleeves and crank out some great food. Now that we have children of our own, Amy and I like to host a few family meals around the holidays, and we're proud of the new traditions we've created. While I can't eat as much as I used to, I do love spending time with our families with a kitchen full of food. Here's a sample menu from one of our holiday get-togethers. It combines some of the traditional holiday flavors with a few little twists. Much of the menu can be made ahead of time, leaving you more time to spend with the family.

Shiitake Gravy

2 cups shiitake mushroom, stems removed & chopped
¾ cup mushroom stock
¾ cup half and half
½ onion, diced
3 cloves garlic, minced
⅓ cup all-purpose flour
salt and pepper, to taste
nutmeg, to taste

In the skillet used for the Turkey Rouladen, sautee onion and garlic in the residual butter.

Toss the mushrooms in the flour until just covered, shaking off any excess. Add floured mushrooms to pan and sautee for about a minute.

Add mushroom stock and use a wooden spoon to really work loose any bits stuck to the bottom of the pan. Add ½ and ½. Season with salt and pepper and a little grated nutmeg.

If sauce is too thick, add a touch more stock. If it's too thin, keep it on low heat for a few minutes to let it reduce.

Cranberry Orange Sauce

Kick the can! This year, forget the "canberry" sauce and make it from scratch. Your guests will thank you.

12 ounces fresh or frozen cranberries
1 cup cane sugar
1 cup orange juice
1 orange, zested, peeled, and chopped
1 teaspoon orange flower water

Place all ingredients in a sturdy, medium pot and bring to a boil. Reduce heat and cook for 10-12 minutes. Remove from heat and let cool to room temperature. Once cooled, place cranberry sauce in the refrigerator to chill. Best if made several days in advance.

Turkey Rouladen with Hazelnut-Shiitake Stuffing

This dish has all of the flavors of the holidays rolled up in a neat little package. You can make the Rouladen the night before and just cook them off the day of your family gathering.

½ cup hazelnut, chopped
2 cups bread, torn
3 tablespoons unsalted butter
⅔ cup onion, diced
2 cups shiitake mushroom, diced
1 cup celery, diced
1 teaspoon garlic, minced
½ teaspoon dried thyme
½ teaspoon ground coriander
1 teaspoon fresh sage, minced
2 teaspoons sea salt
½ teaspoon ground white pepper
1 cup mushroom stock
2 whole eggs
1 pound turkey breast cutlets, pounded
1 cup all-purpose flour
3 tablespoons butter
3 tablespoons olive oil

Make a simple mushroom stock by adding all of your shiitake mushroom stems, onion skins and roots, and celery scraps to a pot and covering with cold water. Bring to a boil, then reduce heat and let simmer while you assemble the rest of the dish.

Toast the hazelnuts in a large, dry skillet until the whole kitchen smells irresistibly nutty and the nuts are dry and crunchy. Remove from the pan and pulse them in a food processor until coarsely chopped. Remove and reserve.

Take slices of good bread (like hearty farm bread or a baguette) and pulse in the food processor until you have 2 cups of chopped and torn bread. It's ok to have a few larger pieces.

Add the butter to your large skillet over medium heat then add onion, shiitakes, celery, garlic, thyme, coriander, sage, sea salt, and white pepper. Cook about 4-5 minutes until the onions and celery turn slightly translucent. Spoon mixture into a large mixing bowl.

Add bread and hazelnuts to the cooked mixture and stir to thoroughly combine. Strain out 1 cup of the simmering mushroom stock and add to the mixture. Let mixture cool for a couple of minutes before adding in the two eggs. (If you stir in the eggs while the mixture is too hot, you'll get bready scrambled eggs!)

Using a meat mallet, pound turkey cutlets until they're evenly thin. Season cutlets with a little salt and white pepper.

Arrange the cutlets so that you have 4 portions that are about the size of a letter envelope. You may have to overlap a couple of smaller pieces, but that's just fine. Add a line of stuffing in the middle of the 'envelope' and fold the front edge of the turkey over the stuffing. Using a gentle rolling motion, roll the turkey over until you've formed a uniform roll. Carefully dust each roll with flour.

Add the olive oil and remaining butter to a large skillet over medium heat. When the butter's melted, carefully add your turkey parcels. Brown on each side then move skillet to a 375 ° F oven for about 8 minutes.

Remove from oven and slice each roulade before service. Serve with Shiitake Gravy and Cranberry-Orange relish.

Spiced Brussels Sprouts

When I was a kid, the very mention of Brussels sprouts made me physically gag. I'd say that I hated them, but I don't think the word 'hate' quite expresses the full depth of the loathing I felt toward those evil green little sprouts. I would have to wash each bite down with a mouthful of Coca-cola, swallowing them like you would a foul-tasting pill. I've spoken to several people with similar childhood Brussels sprout trauma. But I'm living proof that your taste buds mature as you grow older. The little green globes that used to give me nightmares are now one of my favorite vegetables. Brussels sprouts are naturally high in sulfur, and that bitter sulfur comes out when you cook the sprouts too long. So the trick is to just cook them until they're tender and then serve them immediately. If you think you still hate Brussels sprouts, try this recipe and see what you think. You may be surprised to find yourself actually enjoying them.

1 pound brussels sprout, halved
⅓ cup water
3 tablespoons unsalted butter
½ teaspoon garam masala
¼ teaspoon cumin, ground
¼ teaspoon turmeric, ground
½ teaspoon sea salt, to taste
1 tablespoon cane sugar

Cut the ends off of the Brussels sprouts and half them lengthwise. Put sprouts in a microwave-safe glass bowl and add the water. Cover bowl with a microwave-safe plate and microwave for 4 minutes. This will par cook the sprouts. Carefully remove the plate (steam burns are wicked) and drain the sprouts.

In a medium skillet, melt the butter over medium heat. When melted, add garam masala, cumin, turmeric, sugar, and salt and stir to combine. Add sprouts and toss to coat in spiced butter. Reduce heat and cook for another 2 minutes. Sprouts should still tender, but still have an internal bite to them.

Grandma Grace's Cranberry Orange Cake

Amy's Grandma Grace made this a part of her holiday tradition for probably 40 years and I'm sure it'll become a part of yours. The addition of orange juice makes the cake incredibly moist, and the cake is best if you make it a few days in advance. The trick is keeping yourself from eating it before the holidays, so I advise you make two: one for you, and one for your family.

2 ¼ cups sifted all purpose flour
2 cup sugar
¼ teaspoon salt
1 teaspoon baking soda
1 teaspoon baking powder
1 cup chopped walnuts
1 cup diced dates
1 cup fresh or frozen cranberries
grated rind of two oranges
2 eggs, beaten
1 cup buttermilk
¾ cup vegetable oil
1 cup orange juice

Preheat oven to 350° F. Sift together flour, 1 cup of sugar, salt, baking powder, and baking soda. Stir in nuts, dates cranberries, and orange rind. In a separate bowl, combine eggs, buttermilk, and oil, then add to the flour and fruit mixture. Pour into a well-greased bundt pan and bake for one hour, or until a toothpick inserted comes out clean. Remove from the oven and let cool until lukewarm. Remove the cake and place it on a rack over a wide dish. Combine orange juice and remaining 1 cup sugar and pour it over the cake. Take the collected drippings and pour over again until most of the juice has been absorbed. The cake will keep in the refrigerator up to 2 weeks if wrapped in foil, but I doubt it'll last that long!

Pumpkins and other Winter Squash

Pumpkins and their winter squash cousins (gourds, melons, pumpkins, squash, and cucumbers are all in the cucurbit family) are so versatile and provide a ton of nutrients your body can utilize to bolster your immune system. Before the days of refrigeration and imported goods, pumpkins and winter squashes provided nutrients that simply couldn't be found in other foods in the winter months, like Beta-carotine, vitamin C, vitamin A, potassium, selenium, and folic acid. Even better than that, they're delicious!

For the most part, pumpkins, acorn squash, butternut squash, turban squash, and the like can all be used interchangeably and complement each other well. You can steam them, but I prefer to roast them in the oven with a drizzle of olive oil and a pinch of sea salt. If you plan on mashing them, leave them in their skins and simply spoon out the soft flesh when they've had a moment to cool. If you plan on serving large pieces of roast squash or pumpkin, take the time to peel it before roasting, but be careful! A vegetable peeler won't do much on a thick skinned squash, so get out your sharp knife and watch those fingers. Once peeled, cut the pieces into roughly the same size so that they will roast evenly in the oven.

Here's a quick and easy recipe for roast squash or pumpkin, or both! Feel free to spice it up any way you like.

Simple Roasted Winter Squash

4 cups pumpkin and/or winter squash, peeled, seeded, and cubed
2 tablespoon olive or avocado oil
1 tablespoon roast pumpkinseed oil
(optional, but delicious!)
1 tablespoon honey or molasses
2 teaspoon sea salt
1 teaspoon coriander
1 teaspoon cumin
1 teaspoon cinnamon
pinch of cayenne or white pepper

Simply toss all the ingredients together until each piece of pumpkin/squash is coated and place on a roasting pan lined with parchment paper or foil. Roast at 400° F until just knife tender, about 15-20 minutes depending on the variety of pumpkin/squash you use. Any leftovers can be made into a simple soup or mashed and served as a side dish. Enjoy!

Pumpkin Tabbouleh with Pumpkin Butter Vinaigrette

I love tabbouleh, but you can burn out on the same old recipe after awhile. This is just a variation on the original that incorporates the flavors of pumpkin on several levels.

1 cup Bulgur Wheat
1 2/3 cups boiling water
1 cup fresh, chopped parsley
½ cup fresh, chopped mint
1 cup red onion, diced
1-2 cups diced pumpkin or squash, roasted until tender
sea salt/pepper to taste
3 tablespoon roasted pumpkin seed oil
1 tablespoon pumpkin butter
⅓ cup olive oil

Combine bulgur and boiling water in a large bowl. Cover, and set aside to soak for about an hour.

Add oils, onions, parsley, mint, pumpkin, and pumpkin butter. Toss to combine. Season to taste with salt and black pepper. Cover, and refrigerate until chilled. The flavor of the tabbouleh will improve over time, usually best after a night in the refrigerator. Garnish with roasted pumpkin seeds for a little crunch.

Inspiration from Out of the Blue

I grew up about 40 miles from Blue Ridge, Ga., but honestly never paid it too much attention. There was a nice little pet shop where my father and I would go on rainy days to buy fish for our numerous aquariums (fish enjoy a good rainy day), but beyond that, Blue Ridge was just another sleepy North Georgia whistle stop. In truth, I always felt I was rescuing the fish from their mountain captors, explaining to them through the thin, clear walls of their plastic bags that while Jasper was still in the mountains, they were going to live in a restaurant. What an odd journey those fish must have had, traveling from Africa or South America or Asia just to end up on another journey from Blue Ridge to Jasper in a southbound diesel Mercedes wagon.

I forgot about Blue Ridge for about seven or eight years. I was living in the shadow of Atlanta, pursuing academia and a girl named Amy. The drive to Blue Ridge from Atlanta just seemed unfathomable at the time, and there were plenty of good aquarium shops in the metro area, and so the city simply fell off of my radar. In my absence, Blue Ridge evolved into something quite special, emerging from its slumber with an impressive sense of self-pride. When life pulled me back to Blue Ridge, I felt instantly connected, walking through the town with a latte in hand like a local in some European city.

I'd heard about a new gourmet shop called Out of the Blue and, like a salmon swimming upstream, I found the place instinctively. Once inside, I was nearly overwhelmed. The store is a culinarian's playground, each shelf alive with inspiration in a bottle or a jar. But the most impressive thing about Out of the Blue is not what's on the shelves, but rather who put them there. Sarah Auman is a force of nature and within minutes of our introduction, a rare friendship was born. Flitting through the store like a caffeinated hummingbird, Sarah's energy and enthusiasm are both contagious and inspiring. She has amassed a unique collection of food, wine, and all-around fine living items from around the world and from right around the corner.

Until you can make it to Out of the Blue and see the shop in person, be sure to check them out online at www.outofzbleu.com And when you do finally make it to Blue Ridge, give Sarah a hug for me and then load up on a whole bunch of inspiration.

The Woodbridge Inn

If you ever find yourself in north Georgia, please stop by and visit our family restaurant in downtown Jasper. The Inn was built by James Lenning after returning from the California gold rush in the 1800's and used to be a favorite vacation spot for wealthy Floridians trying to escape their summer heat. There are all sorts of interesting things about the Inn, things which I hope to compile in a book one day. But for me, the history that really matters at the Inn is my own. It was my playground, my boot camp, my sanctuary, my first job, my hardest job ... my home. Come and find out for yourself why the Woodbridge Inn is north Georgia's original dining destination. You'll cross that bridge when you get there ...

And now a word from my soapbox:

If you can't make it to the Woodbridge Inn, seek out your local, family-owned and operated restaurants. The proliferation of mega-chain restaurants has seriously threatened the livelihood of the nation's best eateries. I'm not saying that all national chain restaurants are inherently bad, but if you fall in with the herd and only eat at those cookie-cutter, super-predictable operations, you're cheating yourself. Wherever I travel, I make it a point to get away from the highway, drive into the downtown area and find out where the locals eat. These are places established by people who are passionate about their restaurants, from the food, to the service, to the relationships...from beginning to end. Support your local restaurants. They're depending on you.

Feeling Spicy

What began as a little kitchen experiment in my home one Sunday afternoon has turned into somewhat of a cottage industry. I'd been playing around with trying to create a rub for grilled meats that was both sweet and savory without being as salty or cloying as many of the ones I'd tried previously. When I finished mixing my first batch of Honey Buzz, I couldn't stop eating it! It went through a few minor modifications to reduce the heat without losing the distinctive flavors of smoked paprika and chipotle powder, but the final product is exactly what I'd hoped it would be.

Once Honey Buzz was perfected, my ever-active brain kept throwing spices together and now I have a whole line of spice blends and a barbecue sauce in the works. You can find them in a growing list of gourmet shops and grocery stores. And if you can't find them in your favorite shop, tell them to get them! Of course, you can always order them online from my Web site at www.hanscooks.com

Cajun Joe - a spicy, low-salt blend used for blackening meats or seasoning vegetables, potatoes or gumbo.

Honey Buzz - with honey powder, smoked paprika, and orange peel, Honey Buzz is a sweet, smoky rub that's good on everything from chops to popcorn.

Out of the Blue - I use this in nearly everything, Ouf of the Blue is a seasoned sea salt blend with lavender flowers, corriander, and white pepper. Excellent with pasta, grilled veggies, or as a finishing salt for fish and eggs.

Sugar Baby - my kids' favorite! Sugar baby is aromatic blend of raw turbinado sugar spiked with cinnamon, ginger, and cardamom; perfect for baked goods, fruit, or Fairy Toast

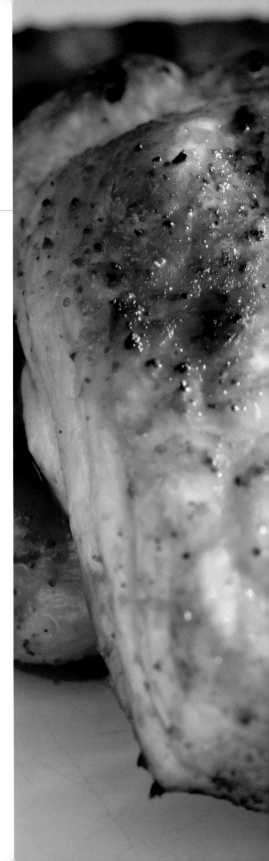

Special Thanks

Family - Amy, Finn, Ella, Joe, Brenda, & Sonja

Wolfgang, Putzi, Tobi, Meike, Klaus, Daggi, Ralph, Lutz, Karsten, Claudia, Petra, Margit, Sybille, Michael, Lydia, and the rest of my German family.

ETC – Huitt Rabel, Adam Chastain, Chad Crowe, Chad Luther, Anna Moore, Erika Watkins, Roger Newton, Phil Herrington, Danny Hensley, Karen Dey-ton, Steven Hames, Hannah Towns, The Harrison Family, Roger Futch, and the rest of my ETC Family.

GPB – Nancy Hall, Bob Olive, Carol Danford, Carol Fisk, Ashley Wilson, Lew Breeding, Darrel Watley

Friends – Sarah Auman, Richard Kirk, Kasra Ghanbari, Leila Weiser, Kevin & Laura Maguire, Brad Mears, Sean Curran, Billy & Rhetta Mears, Ron and Don Bertram, Patrick Moore, Clive Barker, Robb Humphreys, Ludlow Porch & Nancy Hanson, Toren Anderson, Blake Warren, Lorrie Bryan, Joe Mcutcheon, Dan Smith & Steve McDonough, Michael Thomas, Eric Warren, Susannah Locketti, Brook Harlan, Harmony Marceau, Brett Brooks, Roy Robbins, Brook Slane, Dee & Dick Howe, Rebecca Bryan, Sonja Skarstedt, Marion Smith, Lorrie Bryan, Amber & Jeff Mette, Joe McCutchen, Town and Country Furniture, Travis Davis, Geneva Sewell, Marc Summers, Gordon Elliot, Bruce Seidel, Bob Tuschman, Momoko Nakamura and the rest of Food Network friends, Julie Gurovitsch, Jeannette Restivo, Neil Regan, Margery Baker-Riker, Bob Kirsh, John Silk, Cherie Martin, Jim Jones and Family, Judy Dodd, Josh Rasco, Ben Brown, Greg Lewis, Derek Haller, the Hesters, the Landrums, the Johnsons, the Picketts, my wonderful neighbors, and the rest of you … you know who you are.

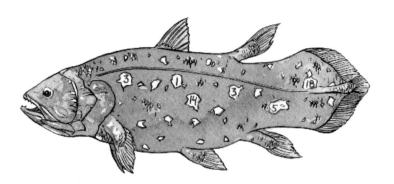

Medical – Dr. Wayne Hoffstetter, Dr. Peter Pisters, Dr. Jaffer Ajani, Dr. Frank Lopez, Tammy Lowe, Dr. R. Martin York, Dr. Carl McCurdy & Staff, Linda Pataki, Madonna Berry, Carolyn Helmer, Dr. Roman Skoracki, Dr. Frederick Schwaibold, Kai Brown, the Jasper Drug Store, Jim Zember, Kathy Newman, Stephanie Braatz

Graphic Innovations - Graphic Innovations, LLC- Mark Waddell, Jon Jones, David Bailey, Kevin Powell (layout and graphic design), Tammie Chastain (project manager)

Photography - Amy & Hans Rueffert, with additional shots from my parents, Wolfgang Rüffert, Chad Crowe, Brad Mears, and Huitt Rabel

Editor: Lorrie Bryan, Rich Miller, Kasra Ghanbari

media relations
Toren Anderson Media
Atlanta   New York   The Low Country
toren@torenanderson.com
770 591-8191
770 928-3635 facsimile
www.torenanderson.com

WEBSITES:

www.hanscooks.com

www.amyrue.com

White Oak Pastures
www.whiteoakpastures.com

Sweet Grass Dairy
www.sweetgrassdairy.com

Flat Creek Lodge
www.flatcreeklodge.com

Out of the Blue
www.outofzbleu.com

The Woodbridge Inn
www.woodbridgeinn.net

Persimmon Creek Vineyards
www.persimmoncreekwine.com

Circle R Beef Jerky
www.circlerjerky.com

ETC TV3
www.northganow.com

Georgia Public Broadcasting
www.gpg.org

R & A Orchards
www.randaorchards.com

Mercier Orchards
www.mercier-orchards.com

Pearson Farms
www.pearsonfarm.com

Harrell Nuts
www.harrellnut.com

Vidalia Valley
www.vidaliavalley.com

Town and Country
www.tccabinfurniture.com

Vatica Vegetarian Cuisine
www.indiagourmet.com

M D Anderson Cancer Center
www.mdanderson.org

Piedmont Hospital
www.piedmonthospital.org

Lance Armstrong Foundation
www.livestrong.org

Georgia Wild Shrimp Council
www.wildgeorgiashrimp.com